HAUNTED SHORES

TRUE GHOST STORIES OF
NEWFOUNDLAND AND LABRADOR

National Library of Canada Cataloguing in Publication

Jarvis, Dale Gilbert
  Haunted shores : true ghost stories of Newfoundland and
Labrador / Dale Gilbert Jarvis.

ISBN 1-894463-54-4

  1. Ghosts--Newfoundland and Labrador. 2. Tales--Newfoundland
and Labrador. 3. Ghost stories. I. Title.

BF1472.C3J37 2004	133.1'09718	C2004-902011-0

Cover photo © Dale Wilson

PRINTED IN CANADA

First printing May 2004
Second printing September 2004
Third printing September 2005
Fourth printing April 2007

FLANKER PRESS LTD.
P.O. BOX 2522, STATION C
ST. JOHN'S, NL CANADA A1C 6K1
TOLL FREE: 1-866-739-4420 TELEPHONE: (709) 739-4477
FAX: (709) 739-4420
INFO@FLANKERPRESS.COM
WWW.FLANKERPRESS.COM

Canada

We acknowledge the financial support of the Government of Canada through the Book Publishing Industry Development Program (BPIDP) for our publishing program.

HAUNTED SHORES

TRUE GHOST STORIES OF
NEWFOUNDLAND AND LABRADOR

Dale Gilbert Jarvis

Flanker Press Ltd.
St. John's, NL
2004

Contents

3. TOKENS, PREMONITIONS, AND GUIDING LIGHTS

4. THAR SHE GLOWS! GHOST SHIPS AND SEA DOGS

5. GHOUL GOULASH: A PARANORMAL MISCELLANY

6. THE FINAL CURTAIN: MURDERS, DEATHS, AND OTHER STRANGE UNDERTAKINGS

INTRODUCTION

Nestled between Breakheart Hill and Bennett's Point, Trinity Bay, is the village of Champney's West. Across the Tickle from Champney's West is Fox Island, which is connected by an isthmus to the mainland. Within the isthmus is a deep freshwater pond, surrounded on either side by stony beaches.

The pond itself is famous for being bottomless, one of several reportedly bottomless ponds in Newfoundland. Of these, the best known is probably Deadman's Pond in St. John's. Local researcher and folklorist Pamela Coristine offers an excellent synopsis of the pond story on her Gothic Lane Web site.

"The legend goes that in the mid-1700s the bodies of executed criminals were displayed on a gibbet at Gibbet's Hill," writes Coristine. "After a time the bodies were cut down, loaded into barrels, weighed down with rocks and rolled into Deadman's Pond. Deadman's Pond was believed to be bottomless, thus ensuring the quick descent into hell of the criminal's damned soul."

A direct portal to Hell in St. John's East? Gothic stuff indeed, and as firm a fixture of St. John's folklore as the miles of tunnels everyone knows are just waiting to be found underneath Water Street. Firm enough in fact to steel the determination of a film crew from Canada's national science fiction and fantasy cable station. They arrived in St. John's one summer as part of a cross-Canada odyssey to explore the unexplained.

After investing in a boat rental and trolling Deadman's Pond, the adventuresome Torontonians demonstrated on national television what every Townie could have told them ahead of time, should they have felt so inclined. Deadman's pond has a bottom. It is not even that far from the surface.

While I personally have not plumbed the depths of the Fox Island pond, something tells me that it probably has a bottom as well. Most of us accept that we live on a spherical planet, and the idea of a pit that truly goes on forever is fantastic. We live in an era where satellite technology allows us to map the ocean's deepest abyss, and unless NASA is holding something back, no direct entranceways to Hell have been discovered.

In spite of scientific advancements and academic treatises, legends like those of Fox Island Pond and Deadman's Pond continue to circulate, be retold, and find their way as "fact" into tourist literature. Why do we continue to tell these tales, and why does the idea of a bottomless lake continue to hold such a grip on our collective imagination?

Part of it must be the fact that Newfoundlanders and Labradorians love a good yarn, even those (or perhaps especially those) known to be less than one hundred percent accurate. But if you will pardon the pun, the reason may lurk deeper still.

Legends and tales of bottomless pits, lakes, and ponds are almost universal. Lake on the Mountain Provincial Park near Kingston, Ontario has a bottomless lake. So does Budapest and the town of Agias Nikolaos in Crete. There is even a Bottomless Lakes State Park near Roswell, New Mexico, which boasts more than one bottomless pond.

These lakes and ponds offer us tantalizing doorways to another realm. Sometimes this other realm is stated as in the legend of Deadman's Pond, and sometimes it is left unsaid. But peering into the reflective surface of a still body of water and wondering what lies beneath provides us with a link to the unexplained. Perhaps this is why they fascinate us. It is not so much that we think they actually are bottomless, but that part of us wishes that they might be.

So too with ghost stories, and indeed, with all things paranormal.

A number of years ago, I met a Newfoundland woman who was experimenting with infrared film. This woman had experienced a number of paranormal encounters in and around St. John's. Using the infrared film, she was attempting to capture images of the spirits she believed she had seen in the area.

Infrared photography uses films that are sensitive to both the light we can see and some of the infrared radiation that we cannot. But does it show ghosts? The photos I saw contained strange, hard-to-define images. Whether these were ghosts, ghouls, or clouds of gas is impossible to say. What can be said for certain is that there are many people who believe that infrared and other types of film can capture things usually not visible to the naked human eye. The interpretation of those images as ghosts seemed to be more a matter of faith or belief than a matter of scientific inquiry.

This belief in ghostly photographs is not new to our haunted shores. In fact, the most famous Newfoundland "ghost photo" is quite historic, and is part of the archival collection of the Anglican Cathedral of St. John the Baptist in St. John's.

The story behind the photograph is quite familiar to many, and has earned a firm place in the oral tradition of the city. According to local folklore, a workman employed on the construction of the Cathedral fell from the heights of the building's south face. The workman died as a result of the fall, and was buried with due ceremony.

When that phase of construction was completed, the workmen involved in the project were lined up at the base of the graveyard to the south of the building. A photograph of the workers in their Sunday best was taken, with the Cathedral in the background. When the photograph was developed, a translucent figure in rough clothes was clearly visible at the end of the line of workers, and a legend was born.

Generations of non-believers, photographic experts and archivists would have you believe it is merely a coincidence. For them it is a double exposure of the sort common in an era when a long exposure time was required when snapping a photo. Julia Mathieson, the wonderful archivist at the Anglican Cathedral, assures me that there is no documentary evidence for a death of any workmen during the construction of the Cathedral. Yet the story persists, and for each skeptic, there is a person who believes in a supernatural origin. As I always say, the decision to believe, or not to believe, lies within yourself.

In preparing this collection of Newfoundland and Labrador ghost stories, I have done my best to present tales that are "true." By this, I mean that I have pulled together a set of stories which are in the public imagination, and which have been collected from archival accounts, published stories, or from personal recollection or experience. They are living bits of Newfoundland and Labrador folklore.

While I cannot prove beyond the shadow of a doubt that any of these tales involve a being or force from another realm of existence, they are not fictional accounts. In each case, they are believed to be true, and have been presented as such. While I have edited narratives that I have collected from people, none of the pieces in this book are works of fiction. Where possible, I have conducted background research on the stories presented, and tried to place the tales in some sort of historical context.

The stories themselves spring from a wide variety of sources. A great number of people have assisted in the preparation of this book, many of them having taken time to tell me or send me stories of hauntings they have experienced or heard about. I have attempted to be true to their tellings, and any errors in the presentation of these stories are my own. Many thanks, in alphabetical order, go to: Geoff Adams, Ed Anderson, Cecilia Baggs, Vicki Barbour, Gordon Bradley, Paul Brake, Debbie Braye, Robert Chafe, Bernie Christopher, Stephanie Courtney, Ray Curran, Juanita Green, Philip Hiscock, Delf Hohmann, Greta Hussey, Michelle Jackson, George Jones, Kelly Jones (thanks for everything!), Bernice

Laurence, Marlene Meade, Margaret "Peg" Moore, Tonya Moores, Robert Parsons, Michael Paul, Janet Peter, Mona Petten, Brian Philpott, Brian Russell, Tina Spencer, Robert E. Tulk, John Warren, David White, Kevin Woolridge, and Ivan Young. If I have forgotten you, thank you too!

There are several other words of appreciation that must be written. During the crafting of this book, my good friend Leida Finlayson passed away after an incredibly brave battle with cancer. Her life, love and friendship will never be forgotten, nor will the support and encouragement she gave me as this book took shape. I will always be in her debt, and I miss her smile and her wit beyond measure.

I also owe a huge thanks to all of those brave souls who have taken part in the St. John's Haunted Hike walking tour since its inception in 1997, and to Mark Scott, Gabe Newman, Steve O'Connell, David Walsh, and Danielle Irvine, my fellow ghoulish guides. Finally, I wish to thank the editorial staff of both *The Telegram* and *The Downhomer*. Many of the stories presented in this book first appeared, in one form or another, in one of those two publications, and the support and encouragement I have received from them has been wonderful. Many thanks as well to Garry, Margo, and the staff at Flanker Press for their support and enthusiasm for this project.

I am fascinated by ghost stories and tales of the unexplained, and I love having people share their experiences. If you know of a haunting in Newfoundland or Labrador, or have experienced something paranormal yourself, please write to me at the address below. Enjoy the book!

Dale Gilbert Jarvis, St. John's, October 2003

Haunted Shores:
True Ghost Stories of Newfoundland and Labrador
70 Fleming Street St. John's, Newfoundland Canada A1C 3A5
info@hauntedhike.com WWW.HAUNTEDHIKE.COM

CHAPTER 1

Unreal Estate: Haunted Homes and Possessed Premises

THE MYSTERIES
OF SUTHERLAND PLACE
KING'S BRIDGE ROAD, ST. JOHN'S

AN INTERESTING GHOST SIGHTING was reported in St. John's in the spring of 1998 at the large Victorian Gothic double residence known as Sutherland Place. Sutherland Place is one of the earliest and largest of the houses that line the historic King's Bridge Road in the east end of the city. King's Bridge Road itself was first opened in the early nineteenth century during the reign of King George III. It connected the British garrison of Fort William in St. John's with Portugal Cove, Torbay, and other nearby outport communities.

In the last two decades of the nineteenth century, right up until the early years of the twentieth century, a number of grand private residences were erected along both sides of King's Bridge Road. Sutherland Place is one of these grandiose homes.

The house dates to 1883, when Mr. William Pitts began to build a double home for himself and his son, the Hon. James S. Pitts. Tragically, William Pitts died in 1884, before the building could be completed. Another son of William's, Arthur, was expected to come over from Britain to share the house with his brother, but he never arrived.

James decided to occupy the north wing of the house, and rent out the south wing to the Outerbridge family. It is said that Sir

1

Leonard Outerbridge observed the Great St. John's Fire of 1892 from his childhood bedroom window on the upper floor. In 1924, Sutherland Place was bought by Sir Edgar Hickman, who later turned the premises into apartments. It is as Hickman Apartments that the building is also commonly known by the older inhabitants of St. John's.

The building has long been associated with some of Newfoundland's most distinguished gentry. James Pitts was appointed to the Legislative Council in 1883, the year construction began on the house, and he later served as a minister without portfolio in four governments. Sir Leonard Outerbridge, who grew up in the house, became the second lieutenant-governor of Newfoundland after confederation with Canada in 1949. Another lieutenant-governor, the Hon. Gordon A. Winter, also lived in the south half of the house as a boy.

Aside from its rich history, the building is an architectural gem, with wonderful peaked bay windows, fine detailing, dormer windows and wrought iron cresting. Sutherland Place also boasts one of the finest local examples of Victorian cast-iron fencing, a type of railing which appears, sadly, to be speedily vanishing.

Sutherland Place is noteworthy not only for its rich architecture and associated history, but also for the fact that it is the site of some of St. John's most dramatic incidences of paranormal activity. Indeed, one of the most recently documented hauntings in St. John's revolves around two of its apartments, located in the top section of the northern half of the building originally owned by the Pitt family.

Toward the end of March 1998, a young woman renting one of these apartments fell asleep one night in the safety of her room. Hours passed, and in the middle of the night she woke up with a start. The young woman, who had gone to sleep without incident, was unexpectedly filled with the overwhelming sensation that someone, or something, was coming after her.

The terrified woman sat bolt upright, and was horrified to see the spectral figure of an old woman standing at the foot of her bed. The crone loomed over her, as if she had been standing, watching the sleeping form. The mysterious visitor featured long black hair,

Sutherland Place, one of St. John's most historic haunted homes (Courtesy of the Heritage Foundation of Newfoundland and Labrador)

and could be seen to be wearing long flowing black clothes. The startled sleeper screamed, threw herself from the bed, past the withered form, and ran to the room of another woman who was sharing the apartment. Too terrified to return to her room, she spent the remainder of a long and torturous night in the same room as her friend.

Readers familiar with similar occurrences might be quick to dismiss this occurrence as nothing more than what is medically known as a hypnagogic hallucination. Excellently documented by David Hufford in his book *The Terror that Comes in the Night*, and more recently by Dr. Paul Chambers in his book *Sex and the Paranormal*, these night terrors are more commonly known as sleep paralysis.

Locally, the phenomenon would be explained away as being nothing more or less than a visitation by that exquisite nocturnal terror known as "The Old Hag." The Hag is part of a nightmare experience usually associated with sleep paralysis. This takes place when the sleeper awakes in a sweat and feels pinned to the bed, as if being ridden by some unexplained force. According to Story, Kirwin and Widdowson's excellent *Dictionary of Newfoundland English*, folkloric remedies for the Hag involve the afflicted party calling out his or her own name backwards. In more dire circumstances, the tortured party was advised to drive nails through a shingle, and to lash the shingle to their breast when they went to bed. When the Old Hag appeared to ride the tormented, the nails would instead torment the Hag! This treatment apparently solved the problem in many instances.

An explanation of the event as merely being a case of sleep paralysis would certainly hold some credence if this sighting was an isolated incident. Our enigmatic bedside companion, however, has been reported on more than one occasion, and seems not to be confined to one particular apartment. The neighbouring suite of rooms has also had nightly visitations of a decidedly supernatural manner.

Late one night, the girlfriend of one of the men renting this second apartment came home after getting off a late shift. The girlfriend worked at one of St. John's many pubs, and was accustomed to getting home quite late on worknights. The barmaid let herself into the apartment, locked the door behind her, and began to walk slowly down the darkened hallway. As she walked past the living room, she was somewhat surprised to observe the dark figure of a woman she did not recognize, sitting by herself on the couch, alone in the shadows.

The girlfriend walked on to her partner's room. Upon entering, she woke him and questioned him about the identity of the stranger on the couch. The man told her there was no one else in the apartment. When she insisted that she had seen an unknown female figure sitting in the living room, they both went back to check. There was no one there. A complete search revealed that the apartment was devoid of any living souls, apart from their own.

The sightings of the ghostly woman in black in the early part of 1998 were, unbeknownst to the residents at the time, precursors of a much more disturbing series of events that would soon unfold within the walls of Sutherland Place.

On April 10, 1998, I visited Sutherland Place for the first time. The apartment I visited lay on the upper storey, and was curiously laid out, no doubt deriving from the fact it was originally a private house which was later converted to apartments.

I walked through the apartment, not exactly certain what to expect. The apartment was very quiet. Despite the fact that it faces King's Bridge Road, a fairly busy street, I was told that a person in the apartment generally cannot hear the traffic. Inside the building for the first time, I could understand better what one tenant had meant by a sensation of an oppressive silence which had engulfed them while in the space.

Using a Sony Mavika digital still camera, I took a number of photographs of the building's interior, including the bedrooms in which night terrors had been experienced, the living room, all the hallways, and the staircase. Examination of these photographs later revealed no anomalous images of any kind. I left a tape recorder running unattended for thirty minutes, in order to see if it would record any noises or voices from beyond the grave. Apart from one thumping noise halfway through the recording, which could have been from a passing truck, the tape offered up little except for the hiss of white noise.

Even though my first visit to the building had uncovered no proof of hauntings, the stories for the collection of apartments did not stop. On March 17, St. Patrick's Day, 2003, I visited the apartments again, this time to talk with a mother and daughter who had lived there for some time, and who had both experienced things out of the ordinary.

One evening, the mother had gone out with a group of friends to see a movie. After the movie, the friends had driven her home. When they arrived, there was a car parked in the driveway, so the friends had to park a little beyond the driveway. This gave the movie-goers seated in their car a perfect view of the windows above them. Had the driver parked any closer to the building, they would not have been able to see the windows of the apartment. The gentleman driving the car asked the mother to point out exactly where her apartment was located, where it began and ended in the building.

The woman pointed out, saying, "You go in these stairs and there is the hallway, and the room that is jutting out is the dining room, and then you come around the corner and see the room with the lights on..." The woman stopped for a moment. "That is the living room, and there were no lights on when I left!" The woman had left no light on in the front room. Because she lived in the house alone, she had a very particular way of leaving on certain hall lights.

Both lights in the window were on. "Well," exclaimed the woman, "someone is taking care of me while I'm out!" She left her friends in the car and went upstairs, and sure enough, the lights were on. This was the beginning of a strange pattern of events. "I could go from room to room," she said, "and if I had to go too far, the light would turn on for me."

Her daughter remembered, "Mother never had to turn lights on in the night. I remember coming in one night, and the overhead light was on. She never turned the overhead on. So I stood in the doorway and I said, 'Now you are showing off!' With that, Mother came down the hallway and asked me who I was talking to. I said to the ghost, because the overhead light is on. Mother just laughed. 'I turned that on!' she said."

Both women laughed, but then the mother added, "We really never did have to turn the lights on. It was the same experience all the time."

The lights seemed to illuminate exactly when they were needed. This was not a frightening type of haunting, and indeed seemed humourous at times. It was, as the mother said, as if someone were taking care of her. Other experiences in the apartment, however, were not pleasant, and lacked the whimsical touch of the ghost that turned the lights on and off.

"I had one experience in bed one night," recalled the mother. "Now, I know there is what they call the Old Hag, and this might have been it, but I was in bed and I was asleep. I found myself fighting for breath, and you feel the weight, there was actual weight on my shoulders, pushing me into the mattress, and into my pillow. I fought, I threw my arms up, and I literally had to fight to get out of that bed. I sat on the edge of the bed, and I was shaking. I really don't think it was a dream. I was too aware of being pushed into the bed. I've had dreams, and I know the difference..."

Because of her experiences while living in Sutherland Place, the mother remains convinced there was some force in the building. "There was definitely somebody in that apartment, there was a spirit in that apartment," she says. "They say ghosts are spirits that are not at peace, and in that apartment there was somebody who was not at peace."

The field investigation and historical research of Sutherland Place offered up few clues to explain the history or cause of the haunting. Its ghostly inhabitant remains a tantalizing figure hovering on the fringes of the unexplained, and a close encounter with one of the supernatural's jealously guarded secrets. Sutherland Place is just one of many sites in the city of St. John's with stories not to be found in history books, and the identity and unknown purpose of its resident spectre may never be revealed. The streets, alleyways and dark corners of St. John's are alive with similar stories of strange events, unexplained phenomena and baffling phantasms. For those who are brave enough to listen, they are stories begging to be told.

A DOMESTIC GHOST
BONAVENTURE AVENUE, ST. JOHN'S

THERE ARE PROBABLY SOME St. John's readers who remember an old mimeographed magazine called *St. John's Woman* which circulated in the early 1960s. The short-lived magazine had an interesting history. It was started by Ron Pumphrey in 1961, containing articles, advertisements, recipes, shopping tips, and a "lonely hearts club" column.

In 1962, the magazine was purchased by Newfoundland author and journalist Cassie Brown. The format then shifted with more emphasis on historical articles and fiction. One article printed in 1962 told the reportedly true tale of a very mischievous phantom who was said to haunt an old house on Bonaventure Avenue. The author was not given, but it is possible it was Cassie Brown, as she wrote many of the pieces.

Sadly the exact address was not given, so it could have been any one of a number of different houses along Bonaventure. It was described as a great old house with a huge front door and a vestibule. This vestibule had a heavy oaken inner door which was always locked with a great key and bolted from the inside. When the family left for the day, they would leave by the back door and lock it from the outside.

The heavy oaken door was involved in one of the ghost's pranks. The custom was to leave the outer door open for the milkman, who would leave a daily quart of milk in the cool vestibule. One day, the husband arrived home to an empty house and found the heavy door unbolted, unlocked, and wide open.

The quart of milk was sitting in the vestibule, but there was no one to be seen. The husband himself had locked and bolted the oak door only a few hours previously. When the rest of the family came home, they denied responsibility for the open door.

Another incident involved a kettle. The father of the house was in the habit of boiling a kettle each morning to make a cup of coffee. One morning he came down to find the kettle boiling away busily on the stove. The kettle contained the small amount of water he used every morning. No one else was awake and had the kettle been boiling for some time, certainly all the water would have boiled away.

While having the kettle ready was at least helpful, other actions revealed that the unknown ghost was something of a prankster. One of the younger men in the house had filled the tub with water in preparation for a bath. Upon leaving the bathroom to fetch a towel, he heard a gurgling noise. Someone had removed the plug from the tub, allowing the water to drain away.

Another brother returned home in the wee hours of the morning ready for bed. Much to his surprise he found his bed completely stripped. The blankets and sheets had been removed, folded ever so neatly, and placed on a chair near his bed.

The most persistent prank involved a clock. Every night the wife of the house would set her alarm clock to go off at seven-thirty. She would then place it on her bedside table, face toward her and within easy early-morning reach. This nightly placement of the timepiece became something of a ritual. Every morning without fail the woman would wake to the alarm, only to find the clock at the other side of the table with the face turned away.

Eventually the woman gave up. She forced her husband to sleep on her side of the bed and moved herself, and the clock, to the other side.

THE GHOST OF BRAZIL STREET
BRAZIL STREET, ST. JOHN'S

F ROM JANUARY 1975 TO MARCH 1977, a man lived in an apartment on Brazil Street, St. John's, high up on the hill just before it meets LeMarchant Road. The previous tenants were friends of the man's, who had been driven out of the apartment because the wife could no longer stand the ghostly manifestations in the place. They blamed these events on a rather sinister painting which had been left behind by some earlier tenant.

The earlier occupants had found the atmosphere sinister and frightening. Objects constantly fell from shelves and walls for no apparent reason, and in spite of the fact that the building stood on solid rock and that there was no moving traffic nearby.

Even though it was extremely difficult to find a vacant apartment in St. John's at the time, particularly a corner one on the top floor of a modern building, nobody else wanted it. The new occupant decided to take a chance and moved in. Upon doing so, he rolled up the suspicious painting and stored it away. He then hung an original oil painting, which belonged to him, upon the wall behind one of the two sofa beds.

The first and most persistent manifestation of the ghostly presence was that the new painting repeatedly fell off the nail upon which it was hung. It would wake the tenant up by crashing onto the electric radiator below. The nail was firmly placed and pointing upwards, so the painting could not have slid off by itself. Most strikingly, the painting always fell down at exactly 3:00 A.M. In the end he was forced to take the painting down.

The gentleman also experienced other curious manifestations, such as a hand, apparently that of a woman's, lightly touching his as he lay in bed. There was also the sound of a handbell being rung. The sound was definitely within the kitchen area of the studio apartment, and could not have come from outside or the next apartment.

He also witnessed a pen jumping at least eight inches into the air, and once saw a kind of formless area of darkness, roughly in the shape of a bat, swoop across the room and vanish into a wall. Even more disturbing was the fact that the man soon started to hear the sound of a woman's voice repeating over and over again "Get away from me!"

THE HAUNTED APARTMENT
LEMARCHANT ROAD, ST. JOHN'S

In DECEMBER OF 1993, a young woman went looking for a new apartment in downtown St. John's. A female friend of hers was visiting, and as the woman was new to St. John's, the friend offered to go with her to help her decide if the apartment was in a good neighbourhood.

The woman had learned of an apartment on the corner of Casey Street and LeMarchant Road, and made an appointment with the landlord to view it. That night, the friend fell asleep on the couch, and rather than wake her, the woman went by herself to look at an apartment. As soon as she saw the apartment, she fell in love with it, and signed the lease on the spot.

Little did she know that while she was away, her friend was having a strange dream. In the dream, the friend was visited by a strange figure. An elderly woman in late-Victorian clothing came to her and showed her the inside of an old building, with high-ceilinged rooms. The Victorian lady told the dreamer "Don't ever step foot in this place; you do not want to go there."

When the sleeper woke she mused on the strange dream for a moment, but then put it out of her mind.

Later, the first woman returned with news of the apartment she had found. Later still, she took the friend to the apartment to show it off. Much to the friend's horror, it was the exact building she had seen in the dream, with the same very high ceilings and period look.

The apartment hunter disregarded the friend's dream, and moved in. After a month or so, a series of odd occurrences began to unfold. One of the first things to happen involved the television and VCR. The woman would be watching television when the VCR would start taping, turning itself on for no reason. This happened several times, without any apparent cause. The machine had never malfunctioned in that way before, and after the woman left the building, it worked perfectly.

The strange events were centred on the living room. The curtains on the window would billow when the window was not open, with no breeze present. At other times a strong perfume would waft through the room; a very strong, heavy scent of lavender like an older woman's perfume. Doors would open and shut for no reason, particularly the door between the living room and bedroom.

One day, as the woman was sitting in a rocking chair in the living room, she felt an unseen force push the chair, setting it rocking. Needless to say, the experience left her feeling profoundly uncomfortable.

The friend who had had the dream heeded the words of the mysterious lady, and never stayed in the apartment. Other people who did come over to visit said they felt something in the apartment, and other visitors were affected in dramatic ways, getting angry and difficult when in the apartment for some time. One guest, sleeping in the living room for three days, underwent a rapid personality change. Over the three-day period the visitor became hostile, confrontational, and eventually got up and left without explanation.

At first the woman was determined to stay in the apartment, but the high rent coupled with the sensation that she was not alone convinced her to seek lodgings elsewhere. Around the time she was getting ready to leave, she was awakened at four in the morning. She woke to the sensation of invisible hands shaking her and the voice of an unseen woman repeating, over and over, "Wake up, wake up."

The woman left the building and she has been untroubled by ghostly forces ever since.

THE GHOSTLY KNOCKINGS OF FORAN'S HOTEL
QUEEN STREET, ST. JOHN'S

THE GHOSTLY KNOCKINGS OF THE FORAN'S HOTEL are the source of one of the oldest continual hauntings in St. John's. There is, however, some historical debate over the exact location of the hotel. In 1883, an elaborate four-storey hotel named the Atlantic Hotel was established by John Foran on Water Street across from King's Beach. The building was at the time one of the grandest in the community, and it remained that way

The old General Post Office in St. John's, one of the suggested locations of the haunted Foran's Hotel (Courtesy of the City of St. John's Archives)

until the Great Fire of 1892 destroyed most of St. John's and gutted the hotel.

Oral tradition, on the other hand, firmly places the building known as "Foran's Hotel" at the intersection of Water Street and

Queen Street, a good six blocks to the west. Folklorist and writer R.J. Kinsella wrote in 1919 that the Foran's Hotel was "situated where the General Post Office now is," which would place it at the second location. It is possible that Foran's Hotel and the Atlantic Hotel were two totally different buildings, as late nineteenth century St. John's was rife with hotels and boarding houses catering to the busy port.

It seems likely given the oral tradition and Kinsella's early twentieth-century version of the following tale that the building in question was located in the second location, and does not refer to the Atlantic Hotel at all.

One night, after all the hotel guests were asleep, a violent knocking noise was heard coming from a vacant room at the top of the building. So persistent was the noise that soon everyone in the building was awakened, but an investigation of the room revealed nothing to account for the clamour.

The noise was not repeated that night, but the next night at the exact same time, the hotel was racked with the same violent knocking. Nothing was found, and the third night, the knocking was renewed, causing great turmoil amongst the guests and lodgers. With the reputation of the hotel close to ruin, the guests were persuaded to stay, and a party was organized to stand watch, with a double guard placed at the room door. That night, mysteriously, the knocking ceased, and was not heard again. The room was closed to the public, memory of the incident faded, and life and business returned to normal.

Several months after the disturbance, an unknown man arrived in St. John's, and made his way to the Foran's Hotel, where he demanded lodging for the evening. At that point the establishment was full, with every room occupied except one. Rather than send the mysterious gentleman to a rival hotel, the staff gave the man the room which had been the epicentre of the psychic disturbance months before. The stranger retired to the room, and later that night, the entire hotel was aroused by the old knocking, this time in a long and insistent outburst of wrath.

Guests and staff rushed to the bedchamber, and upon breaking in found the new lodger, lying on the bed, fully clothed, and cold in death. A doctor was called, who declared that the man had died from massive internal hemorrhaging, but as the corpse was removed for burial the next day, a distinct rapping noise could be heard throughout the apartment, which persisted until the very instant the body was removed from the premises.

The man was never identified, and his body was buried quietly in the old Methodist Cemetery. The room was boarded up, and never used again. The questions that surrounded his strange death were never answered, and today, even the exact location of his grave has disappeared into the mists of time.

As noted by Kinsella, Foran's Hotel was replaced by the old General Post Office building. Eventually this building was demolished in the 1960s and replaced by a modern office tower used as a central postal station by Canada Post. Interestingly enough, stories were in circulation as recently as 1998 that the Canada Post building was haunted. In 1998, it was reported that strange, unexplained knocking noises were heard by postal workers on one of the upper stories.

PETER PAUL AND GOVERNMENT HOUSE
MILITARY ROAD, ST. JOHN'S

THE FIRST PROPER GOVERNMENT HOUSE in Newfoundland was built at Fort Townshend. Today, its original location is marked by a plaque on the east wall of the Central Fire Station on Bonaventure Avenue. The dwelling was finished in 1781, and was originally intended as a summer house for the governors. Reportedly, it was never very comfortable in winter.

This fact may have had something to do with the demise of the first governor to overwinter here in Newfoundland, Francis Pickmore, who died in the building in 1818. It was Pickmore who, according to one popular bit of local folklore, was shipped home to England inside a barrel of liquor.

A later Governor, Sir Thomas John Cochrane, commissioned building plans for a grander and presumably warmer residence on Military Road. Work on the structure started in 1827 on the barrens at the edge of town, to the east of a bog.

When the construction of Government House was finished in 1831, the cost was five times the original estimate. The building itself was a relatively plain Georgian mansion, built of masonry, with a centre block and two wings. The British government took a long hard look at Cochrane's extravagant spending, and punished him by reducing his salary. In spite of the money spent on it, early critics were less than enthusiastic. Historian D.W. Prowse went as far as to describe it as "a huge pile of unredeemed ugliness."

Today trees and gardens surround the exterior. It is this area, the Government House grounds, that is the setting for an old St. John's ghost story.

The grounds of the mansion are said to be haunted by the ghost of a phantom soldier, nicknamed Peter Paul. On occasions, Peter Paul has been sighted walking the tree-lined area between the residence and Military Road. Those who claim to have met him agree that he is usually dressed in a soldier's coat with white trim. He is described as being a tall man, but a clear description of his face has never been made, as each sighting has reported his face hidden by the high collar of his coat.

The ghost's perambulations were noted by several Governors, including Sir Humphrey Thomas Walwyn, who was governor for most of the Commission of Government period, from

1936 to 1946 . One Governor, unfortunately unnamed, had grave doubts about inhabiting a haunted mansion. As the story goes, the reluctant believer was talked into moving in by his much more skeptical wife.

The figure of Peter Paul is thought to be the ghostly remains of an infantryman who lost his life during one of the many battles fought between the French and English. One written account of the haunting hypothesizes that he died in 1770.

An official ceremony at Government House, the grounds of which are haunted by the soldier Peter Paul (Courtesy of the City of St. John's Archives)

If this date is true, Peter Paul would have been killed well before the building of the first Government House at Fort Townshend. However, the site of his demise would have been quite close to the nearby Fort William, which was erected circa 1700.

Perhaps Peter Paul was involved in action during the Seven Years War, which ended in 1763. Toward the end of that conflict a French squadron marched on St. John's. They captured Fort William on June 27, 1762, raided nearby settlements, and immediately set about improving the fortifications. When they surrendered it back to the English on September 18 of the same year, the English found the fort in better condition than it had been when they left!

Sadly, Peter Paul has been less diligent in his guard duty since Confederation, and sightings of him have been few and far between. A better understanding of the circumstances of his life and death must be left either to a diligent military historian, or to a lucky ghost-hunter out for a late- night stroll along Military Road.

THE INSPECTOR GENERAL'S PHANTOM
HARVEY ROAD, ST. JOHN'S

In JULY 2000, A NUMBER OF BUILDINGS were demolished at Fort Townshend to make way for The Rooms, the province's controversial new museum, art gallery and archives. One of these demolished buildings was quite historic—the structure known as the Inspector General's House at 1 Harvey Road. As well as being rich in history, the building was also reportedly haunted.

The house at 1 Harvey Road was constructed in 1895 and was fully in use by 1897. It was of timber construction with a hip roof pierced by three gables, and a fine cut stone foundation.

The building itself was of a fairly unornamented, Queen Anne Revival-style, with classic elements reflected in the use of pediments and corner pilasters. It originally featured ornamental brackets under the eaves, though these were removed sometime after 1970.

The first occupant was John Roche McCowen, born in Kilrush, County Clare, Ireland. He came to St. John's in 1871 to join the Terra

The Inspector General's House on Harvey Road, St. John's, now demolished (Courtesy of the Heritage Foundation of Newfoundland and Labrador)

Nova Constabulary. In 1895, McCowen was appointed Inspector General of the Newfoundland Constabulary and had a house constructed just south of Fort Townshend. The residence was occupied by a number of inspectors general and their families until 1952.

After that time, it was occupied by the Department of Economic Development under Alfred Valdmanis, and also housed

John Roche McCowan and his wife. Did his spirit haunt his former official residence? (Courtesy of the City of St. John's Archives)

the premier's office under Newfoundland premier Joey Smallwood. By 1965, the occupant of the building was the Traffic Court. The front of the building originally featured two large bay windows, which were converted to one larger bay, extending the usable space in the courtroom. While the exact date this change was made is not known, it was most likely done in the late 1950s or early 1960s.

Around 1984, the building was taken over by the Estates Division of the Supreme Court, and was used by the Estates Division until the destruction of the property.

It was during its use by the Traffic Court that rumours of its otherworldly inhabitant began to surface. Workers staying late or coming back at night to finalize reports would often hear the sound of footsteps coming up the basement stairs. There was nobody there.

The noises were so well known and so inexplicable that several employees would not work nights. At other times, strange banging noises were heard emanating from the kitchen, or misty figures were seen from the corner of the eye.

One night, a worker remained in the building quite late. The boss had indicated he might come in to catch up on a few things, so when the woman heard footsteps she assumed it was him.

A shadow passed in front of her open door. The woman called out to the figure, asking for help with a particular file. When she looked up, the figured had stopped, turned sideways and was looking straight at her. The figure was an older man, about five feet, ten inches tall, and was wearing a shocked look on his face. He had white, curly, bushy hair, cut just below the ear, sideburns and a handlebar moustache. He was wearing a dark or black coat with tails, a charcoal- grey waistcoat or vest and trousers that matched. The figure was so solid and so real that the woman could even detect a faint pinstripe on the grey waist coat, and what appeared to be spats!

The shocked woman spoke again to the distinguished older man, but it seemed as if he could not understand her speech. He then vanished before her eyes.

Today, the only thing that remains of this property is the cast-iron gateway visible at street level on Harvey Road. The ghost's former house is gone. But ghosts, it seems, care little for the changes we mortals make to our physical landscape. Perhaps The Rooms will have a ghost of its own, or our mysterious gentleman will continue to climb his staircase and bang around in his kitchen, unaware of the changes around him, a psychic reminder of the history that was bulldozed in the name of progress.

THE MOCKBEGGAR SPOOKS
BONAVISTA, BONAVISTA BAY

THE AREA KNOWN AS MOCKBEGGAR in Bonavista is the home to a number of strange tales. Several of them revolve around what is known as Bradley House on the Mockbeggar Property.

The house itself has a long and interesting history. Jabez Saint built the house in 1871 on property acquired from John H. Warren. It is possible Jabez had help from his in-laws, the Strathies, a well-known family of builders responsible for the construction of many of Bonavista's fine old buildings. The lumber used in the construction of the house is said to have come from an older structure that once stood on this property.

Unfortunately, Jabez went bankrupt in 1879. As he was in debt to Baine Johnston and Company, they seized his property. Fortunately, they allowed him to occupy the house. In 1898, John Roper acquired the property from Baine Johnston and Company, but Jabez Saint was permitted to live in the building until his death in 1903.

The property passed from the Ropers to their son-in-law, Senator Gordon Bradley, one of the original signatories to the Terms of Union with Canada. In 1981, the Bradley Family donated the property to the Newfoundland Government. It was declared an Historic Site in 1988 and was officially opened as a museum in 1990.

In addition to having such a rich history, the Bradley house is said to be haunted. Part of the story comes from a member of the Bradley family, Mr. Gordon Bradley, the son of Senator Bradley. According to him, there were once local rumours circulating that one of the ghosts was a member of the family itself!

Years ago, there were stories told in Bonavista of families from the Mockbeggar area that would pass along that house late at night and see a strange sight. A light would be on in the window, and passersby would be able to peer in and catch a glimpse of Mr. Bradley's grandmother sitting in the rocking chair knitting. Hardly remarkable, you might think, unless you knew that these sightings took place long after the lady had passed away.

Another member of the Bradley family had experiences with ghostly activity inside the building. Mr. Bradley remembered going down to the house one morning a little while after breakfast. After he and his mother had chatted for a bit she said, perhaps a little tongue-in-cheek, "They were at it again last night."

"Who was at what, mother?" asked her son.

"The people who live upstairs," the woman replied.

When he asked what they had been doing last night, she said that she was not exactly sure, as she had not bothered them. She had, however, heard them walking about, talking, singing and having a party, complete with slamming doors. After a while, the phantom party-goers had settled down, and she had been able to go up and go to sleep. They seemed to be friendly ghosts, and the woman was of the opinion that if they did not bother her, she would not bother them.

Other people in Bonavista have had equally strange experiences around the property, and there are many stories about the Bradley house. For example, a white light has been reported burning in the top middle window of the place when it was supposed to be empty.

Some of the sightings are quite recent. During the summer of 1999 a girl who lived near Ropers Lane, along with a friend of hers, took a shortcut. This shortcut took them right past the house. As they drew near they suddenly heard the sound of rattling chains directly behind them. No physical source could be seen. The two girls were terrified and ran to the safety of their homes.

Mockbeggar House in Bonavista is haunted by more than one spirit. (Courtesy of the Heritage Foundation of Newfoundland and Labrador)

When she got home, the girl was told that her own sister had experienced an equally strange event. When the sister had been her age, she had been walking past the rear of the building late one night. As the sister had looked up into the top middle window of the place, she had seen two green eyes peering out at her. The sister claimed to have seen the eerie green eyes on more than one occasion.

The hauntings of the Bradley House, Bonavista may be somehow linked to another mystery of the Mockbeggar property. In the 1920s, under the direction of William Coaker, a canal was dug in the area. As the canal was being dug, a number of coffins were excavated. Then, years later, more coffins were unearthed during the construction of the new bridge across the canal in 1946.

The graves were believed to predate the earliest cemetery in Bonavista, which dated to 1725, and no one knew anything about them. The caskets were found to contain the remains of men, women and children. When they were examined in greater detail, the mystery deepened. It was discovered that the coffins were pegged together instead of being nailed, and that they were made from a wood which the Newfoundlanders did not recognize as a local species.

One theory was that the bodies were French in origin, as the French had been active in the early years of the fishery at Bonavista. Some refuted these claims, arguing that the French had not brought their wives and children with them while exploiting Newfoundland's rich fishing grounds.

The coffins had been buried in the mud, which helped preserve them. Over the years, several homes were constructed over this unusual cemetery, and the identities of the people inside the Mockbeggar coffins were never revealed. The strangers were immortalized in a poem entitled "The Revolt of the Spooks." It is said today that on a windy, stormy night you can hear the sound of singing in a foreign language coming from the site of the old graves.

When the bodies were found, they were described as wearing Puritan-style clothing. Several pieces of cloth were taken from one of the graves. These pieces are now locked away in the town vault, tantalizing evidence which will perhaps someday help solve the mysteries of Mockbeggar.

VICTORIA STATION
DUCKWORTH STREET, ST. JOHN'S

———

LIKE MANY OTHER STREETS in downtown St. John's, Duckworth Street has its own rich history of ghost stories. I have been told that two different buildings across from the War Memorial are haunted, one by the ghost of a woman who has been seen walking down the stairs. Another ghostly woman was reported outside, on the street itself, in 1909.

The most well-known haunting for the street, however, is certainly that of the building that stands on the northeast corner of the intersection of Duckworth and Cathedral Street.

The double house was built in the 1890s for Dr. T.M. Mitchell and Thomas Kavanagh. It sits on the site of the old Scottish Presbyterian Kirk, which was destroyed by fire. Dr.

The old Victoria Station building on Duckworth Street, on the left of the photo here, is one of St. John's most haunted properties. (Courtesy of the City of St. John's Archives)

Mitchell used his half of the building as an office, surgery and residence for over thirty years. Throughout the twentieth century, the building was used by various doctors, including Dr. Bernard Joseph Kennedy, who used the premises as a surgery.

According to a popular local legend, one of the more interesting uses to which the building was put was that of a funeral parlour, although the City of St. John's Archives has no direct evidence of this occupation. Regardless of how the building was used in the past, the undisputed fact remains that this fine old building is haunted by at least one, if not several, phantoms.

Throughout the early 1990s, the building served as the Victoria Station Inn, Restaurant and Coffee Bar. Stories circulate that while Victoria Station was used as an inn, there were several incidents involving visitors from beyond the grave. Indeed, on more than one occasion, guests staying at the inn actually left in the middle of the night, driven out of their rooms by unspecified paranormal activities.

Late one night, one of the staff was working after regular hours, and was alone in the building. The man was working in one of the upper rooms of the structure. As he turned around, he was met with an unexpected and terrifying sight. There, leaning against the mantel, dressed in the finest evening clothes and smoking a pipe, was the figure of a distinguished gentleman. The Victorian gent stood watching the startled employee, and then vanished without a trace.

Stories circulated that the spectre, nicknamed "Jacob" by the staff at the time, was in fact the ghostly remains of the old undertaker, who continues to preside over the former funeral parlour long after his death. Others claim that Jacob is not alone, and that an attractive woman has been sighted standing in the corner of one of the rooms, smiling sweetly before vanishing.

The list of events said to have taken place in the building is long and eerie. Different people have reported suddenly feeling strange sensations while on the ground floor level, while others have encountered spots of cold air. There is another story which tells of a time when the building was closed for the day, and the staff was cleaning up. Suddenly a vase that was on an end table flew across the room and fell to the floor.

HAUNTED PUBS
DOWNTOWN AREA, ST. JOHN'S

THE DUKE OF DUCKWORTH is one of St. John's many fine pubs, and as fine a place as any to whet your whistle and sample one of Newfoundland's locally produced brews. The Duke, however, is also famous for spirits of another kind, as the structure is said to be haunted by a mysterious form that appears in the window above the entranceway, and which has been known to wave a ghostly hand at pedestrians navigating McMurdo's Lane.

The Duke also features the only known local paintings of the Duke's ghost, located to the right of the bar inside. Those of you with keen eyes who visit the Duke, however, will note a slight error in the painting, as the artist has shown the spirit materializing in the window of the building across McMurdo's lane.

Christian's Pub on George Street is another one of the town's haunted pubs. It is the oldest pub on George Street, and indeed, is located in one of the street's oldest buildings. The Christian's ghost is a relatively well-known attraction at the pub, and has even been immortalized on the pub's Web site. The ghost is said to be female, and has been lovingly nicknamed Maggie by the proprietors.

Maggie has been seen to materialize in physical form by several of the staff members, who claim to have seen the figure of a

Christian's Pub, shown here in the 1970s, has a resident spirit nick-named Maggie. (Courtesy of Newfoundland Historic Trust)

woman in a long white dress appear in one of the old church pews on the main floor. Indeed, the proprietors of the public house have hypothesized that the figure of the woman actually arrived at the pub with the pews themselves, which were taken from the old Congregationalist Church on Queen's Road. What a devout Congregationalist churchgoer is doing on George Street, long after her death, is anyone's guess.

In addition to taking up valuable seating space, Maggie has also been known to wreak havoc with equipment behind the bar, and to stomp disapprovingly around the second storey when there is no one actually on the second floor to see her doing so.

THE WHISTLING GHOST
CARTWRIGHT, LABRADOR

In 1998, a man, his wife and infant daughter moved to Cartwright, Labrador, so that he might take up employment there. The community of Cartwright is named for Captain George Cartwright, a merchant and adventurer who lived along the coast for a decade in the late 1700s.

The family lived in the old staff house on what is known as the "Grenfell Grounds." On different occasions, the house had served as clinic and temporary hospital, and as time passed the family began to learn of unusual occurrences that had happened there in the past.

The wife's mother, who was visiting with the family for a while, would always go down to the basement to smoke. She would sit on a bench almost opposite the furnace-room doorway, and told her daughter and son-in-law that more than once she experienced a very peculiar sensation. She said that this caused her to feel very uneasy about the dark entrance to the furnace room.

The laundry room was also on that level and after dark, when someone had to go down there to get laundry, they could never shake the feeling that they were not alone, particularly when ascending the dimly lit, steep staircase. The husband always felt that someone was right behind him, and he would constantly look behind himself as he went up.

One evening the couple were feeding their daughter. The three of them were alone in the house. As they were feeding her, the father began to whistle a song to the girl. But when he stopped whistling, the whistling continued for a very short time from somewhere else in the house. Both the wife and the husband clearly heard this, and there was no mistaking the sound.

While no fully satisfactory explanation for the ghost on the Grenfell grounds has ever been found, it may have something to do with a tragic death at the Grenfell Mission boarding school property in the 1930s.

The boarding school building had been erected to care for sixty people including the staff, a large group of children, and the hospital patients. In June of 1934, the Mission was struck by a major disaster. A fire erupted in the building, and the entire structure was quickly destroyed, leaving only the foundations and the chimney behind.

That October, Dr. Richard Light wrote up his impressions of Cartwright for the New England Journal of Medicine. He noted that one of the sad results of the mission fire was the death of a patient. The patient was a girl of seventeen who had been in the recovery stages of scarlet fever.

Dr. Light wrote that "her remains were discovered some weeks later, and the funeral arranged. The Grenfell doctor was requested to serve as pallbearer; he marched at the head of the procession, bearing in his hands a small box containing the few bones recovered. Behind him in slow procession filed Cartwright's seventy-two inhabitants; all, except one man who remained to toll the bell over the silent marchers, until the ceremony was ended."

The funeral was presided over by an elderly judge by the name of Murphy who read several Bible passages while the coffin was lowered into its resting place. Dr. Light recorded that it poured rain that day, and the burial plot was filled with water before the interment was completed.

The Grenfell Mission staff house in Cartwright, Labrador, is the site of ghostly whistling. (Courtesy of David Gatehouse)

The Grenfell grounds in Cartwright saw many a death from disease and injury over the years, but it is hard to imagine a more tragic death or sadder funeral than that of the girl who perished in the flames of 1934. Perhaps her spirit is the one that lingers, haunting the living with a strange whistling from beyond the grave.

THE PRIEST AND THE LIBRARY
GOULDS, AVALON PENINSULA

I*T HAS LONG BEEN REPORTED* that the old Father Slatery library of St. Kevin's Elementary School in the Goulds, south of St. John's, was haunted by the same priest for whom it was dedicated. As a child, one local resident was present during two sightings. Both occurred during the night. The first involved some students taking part in a concert who, fooling around, went up to the library.

Reportedly, the students headed to the library in order to get a good scare. They apparently got one, and came running down the stairs frightened because they had seen the priest. A skeptic could say that this was just the children making up stories, but the library has a long reputation in the community for being haunted.

The local man's second ghost sighting took place one night when he was walking alongside the school with some friends. The library has one lonely window on the side they were on, and it always gave the young man a chill to walk by it. On this particular night he looked up and saw that the curtain was closed. When he looked back, it was opening by itself.

Not staying long enough to ask questions, the boy ran home. The movement could easily have been caused by a night janitor, but why would a janitor, working late at night, not have turned on the lights?

THE BARNES ROAD BOOJUM
BARNES ROAD, ST. JOHN'S

In OCTOBER OF 2002, I HEARD A STORY from a man who had grown up in the downtown area of St. John's. He and his family had lived on a street running off Military Road in the centre of the city. Several members of the family had felt a presence in the house, and the matriarch of the clan had even felt the eerie sensation of being bumped into by the resident spirit.

The dwelling was an old house, three storeys high, and typical of those in the downtown core. Up on the top floor of the house were a couple of spare rooms which the family did not use a great deal.

One of the rooms was quite large, more or less empty, and was used for storage.

There were seven in the family, and with that many people in one house, empty rooms did not stay empty forever. When he got into his teenage years, one of the sons commandeered the top floor room for his own use. The son experienced nothing out of the ordinary in his time spent there. Later on, the mother decided she was going to use the room as a sewing room, where she could sit and sew, and do the ironing.

Unlike her son, she began to realize she was not always alone in the room. On many occasions when she was in the room, she felt something of a presence. Whatever it was, it was always unseen. The spirit and the sense of discomfort it lent to the top floor always caused her to feel more than a little uncomfortable in the space.

One day while doing her ironing, the lady was nudged, pushed by an invisible figure. The woman put down the hot iron, backed away from her chores and said, "OK! I'm going!"

The couple who owned the house were both skeptical people, and were known to be very down- to-earth sorts, especially the father. He thought his wife was crazy, and decided to check it out for himself and spend some time in the room. He was not one who had any time for nonsense, and wanted to put the rumour that the house was haunted to rest.

To prove there was nothing supernatural in the room, the father spent a bit of time there, reading and whatnot. Finally one night he came downstairs, looking rather white in the face.

"I'm going to tear out the ceiling in that room" he exclaimed.

When questioned, he said nothing. Something frightening had obviously happened, but the man refused to tell his family what had transpired in that mysterious room. He was, however, quite serious about tearing out the ceiling. Always the skeptic, he felt that there might be a rat or some other flesh-and-blood creature moving around above the plaster.

True to his word, he hauled out the ceiling, stripping away the laths and plaster. Carefully, he investigated the newly opened space. Much to his chagrin, he found absolutely nothing. There were no signs of rats or other beasties, and nothing to account for whatever he had felt, heard, or witnessed in the room.

The ceiling was repaired, with new plaster and paint. Before long, the room was back to normal, or, as the case may be, back to the paranormal. For no sooner was the ceiling replaced, than the family began to feel the same eerie sensations yet again. The ghostly presence was felt for years afterwards, and eventually the family moved away. For all we know, the phantom could be there still.

CHAPTER 2

What is this Figure Before Me?

THE GHOST CHOPPER
BARACHOIS BROOK, ST. GEORGE'S BAY

ONE OF THE MOST FAMOUS GHOST STORIES in Canada is that of the Dungarven Whooper from the Miramichi region of New Brunswick. The Whooper is said by some to be the ghost of an ill-fated logger who died years ago during the breakup of a log jam, and his whooping call is said to still resound through the woods along the Miramichi River.

Not to be outdone, Newfoundland can boast its own ghostly logger. Although the exact circumstances of his demise are lost in the mists of time, he can still be heard in the woods near Barachois Brook. And where the Dungarven Whooper is content to shout his way through the afterlife, our Newfoundland ghost is a harder-working sort of spirit, busily chopping away in death just as he did in life.

It is his chopping in fact that distinguishes the ghost, for he has never been seen by mortal eyes. Mortal ears, however, are another matter. Many visitors to the woods have stopped and listened as his ghostly axe bites deep into another tree somewhere just beyond the next stand of timber.

Mr. Ivan Young, of Barachois Brook, remembers hearing the ghost chopper himself when he worked in the logging camps in 1948 and 1949. He was working for Fred Butt, cutting wood to make barrels used for pressing herring. The camp was near Little River and at that point was a sizeable operation, with choppers, teamsters, mill workers and people hauling the barrels out to the station. This meant around fifty to fifty-five men working long days, plus one ghost who would chop all night long.

The ghost would start chopping around seven o'clock. According to reports, it was a quite spirited spectre and would work all night. As soon as it got daylight, it would quit. Amazingly, it would only chop about two or three times, a sound which would be followed by the noise of a huge tree falling in the forest. If someone tried to walk out toward the apparition it would move on, circling round and round and round, always a couple steps ahead of its pursuer.

While Mr. Young was working at the camp, the owners bought a diesel engine which didn't always work the way it should have. A repairman was sent in from St. John's and he too heard the strange chopping. When the ghost started with his axe, the repairman asked what it was, and was told it was the ghost chopper. The skeptical townie refused to believe it was true, so Ivan Young and a fellow named George Alexander put on a lantern and took him out on snowshoes.

The trio followed the noise of the axe, and as they went around, the sound of the trees falling was always just ahead of them. From the noise of the fall, it seemed like the trees being cut were huge, but where a living man would take at least a half-hour to cut through one of the trees, the phantom woodsman did the job in no more than five or six hearty chops.

Of course, the repairman was convinced that it was someone playing a joke on him. In the morning, after the engine was up and running, he put on his snowshoes and followed the previous night's snowshoe tracks through the woods. Not one tree was cut. And sure enough the next night the chopping resumed. Engine repaired, he departed for St. John's a little more open- minded than when he arrived.

In time the demand for herring lessened and the cooperage closed. This forced the closure of the lumber camp, but not before at least one lucky man had an unnaturally cold form crawl into bed with him early one morning! Even after the camp closed the ghost chopper kept going strong, working away through many winters.

In 1979, Nora Healey Keegan wrote her book *Footprints in the Sand*. In the book she devoted a chapter to what she referred to as "The Phantom Woodchopper." According to her, this was a mysterious phantasm who worked the woods of Steel Mountain, which lies several miles to the northeast of St. George's. Her brother and father had gone out one crisp, frosty evening after rabbits and had heard the distant sound of steel on wood. After a moment's terror, the two men decided to track the noise to its source. Like others before them, they hiked along following the chopping, sometimes near, sometimes distant, without ever catching a glimpse of the elusive figure.

Even after over fifty years the ghost is still hard at work, and has been heard as recently as into the late 1990s. A man went into the woods to help his brother bring back wood he was cutting, and he followed the sound of a ringing axe around in circles. The ghost led him on a merry chase, and if the man hadn't known the country, he would have been lost.

There are some who claim to have seen trees fall under the logger's axe, but this is a very rare occurrence. Furthermore, those who have gone out in the summer have not heard a thing. But if you wait till next winter and venture into the woods near Barachois Brook, you too might hear the distant chop, chop, chop of the phantom woodsman.

ANNE PEARL'S GHOSTLY RIDE
MOUNT PEARL, AVALON PENINSULA

W HEN ONE THINKS OF HISTORIC SITES and places in Newfoundland and Labrador, one community that you might not place at the top of the list is Mount Pearl. In truth, however, Mount Pearl not only has some fascinating history, it is home to one of the finest and most dramatic ghost stories in the province.

The ghost story involves a woman whose maiden name was Anne Hawkins. Ms. Hawkins was the daughter of a wealthy merchant and supplier to the Kensington Palace. In 1826, Anne, a young debutante, met a thirty-seven-year-old bachelor named Commander James Pearl. By this point, James had already had an intriguing and distinguished career.

A native of Kelleys Cove, Yarmouth County, Nova Scotia, James Pearl joined the British Navy in 1801 at the tender age of eleven. He graduated from the Royal Naval Academy in 1805 and was stationed to the HMS *Neptune*. The *Neptune* joined with other ships under the command of Admiral Horatio Nelson off the coast of Trafalgar and engaged the French.

The Admiral's ship, HMS *Agamemnon*, took several blows, losing her forward spar, and Nelson was mortally wounded. The *Neptune* escaped the first French broadsides, and Pearl moved his ship into the middle of the fleet with guns blazing, causing serious losses to the French fleet.

Pearl went on to serve in numerous other notable naval battles, and received a severe head wound while steering a fireship in a manoeuvre to break the French fleet in the Basque Roads engagement. When a piracy war broke out in the Burmese area of the Bay of Bengal in 1824, Pearl was again in the thick of the fray.

It was when James returned to England from the Bay of Bengal that he met Anne Hawkins. According to one historian, James was a very eligible bachelor, with many affluent and influential friends, including the writer Thomas Carlyle, the poet Robert Browning and his wife Elizabeth Barrett Browning. He was also quite a sportsman and loved yachting and polo. In particular he enjoyed horseback riding, a passion he shared with young Anne.

James and Anne began courting seriously. King William IV and his wife Adelaide knew both parties, and when James and Anne announced their intended union, the King and his Queen stated they were delighted with the match.

The couple were married in the spring of 1827, the same year that James retired from His Majesty's Navy. Anne and her new husband settled down in Kensington in wedded bliss.

In 1829, Anne and James sailed aboard the HMS *Britannia* from Liverpool to St. John's, carrying an order from the Colonial Secretary of State bidding the then Governor Cochrane to grant him 1,000 acres of Crown Land in recognition of his meritorious service for King and Country. Pearl's grant was soon cut in half, the other portion going to two Scottish immigrants. Despite his displeasure with this decision, Pearl named his estate Mount Cochrane in the governor's honour.

Upon their arrival in Newfoundland, Anne and James stayed for a while in St. John's. While there, they lived with James's sister and his brother-in-law, George Blamey. As soon as the frost lifted in February of 1830, Pearl began clearing land. By the time he was knighted by Queen Victoria in 1838, Sir James Pearl had developed Mount Cochrane into a thriving farm area which supplied some of nearby St. John's with livestock, fruits and vegetables. Out of his own funds James built the road which became Old Placentia Road.

Within ten years, the Pearl estate included roads, their home, and several hundred acres of farmland. James's relationship with Governor Cochrane, which had started off badly with Cochrane's refusal to give the Pearls their full estate, quickly deteriorated. Eventually, James became so infuriated with Cochrane that he had the property renamed Mount Pearl.

Part of the Mount Pearl farm included grounds set aside specifically for horse racing. The Pearls oversaw the construction of

While Lord Pearl rests quietly in the old Anglican Cathedral graveyard, his wife has been known to appear at their old estate astride a phantom horse. (Courtesy of the Heritage Foundation of Newfoundland and Labrador)

a benched gallery for spectators and a rounded track, which drew many people. Both Anne and James were noted for their love of horses and riding, a passion that would figure strongly in events yet to unfold.

Anne's husband died suddenly at the Pearl estate on January 13, 1840, aged fifty years. His funeral took place on Friday, January 17 from Exmouth Cottage, the residence of E. Moore of Her Majesty's Customs. Lord Pearl was laid to rest in the Anglican Cathedral churchyard in downtown St. John's. Over the past century and half, most of the tombstones which once lined that yard have vanished, leaving but a few markers remaining. One of these is the tombstone of Sir James, and it is still visible for those who care to seek it out.

On August 1, 1840, several months after her husband's death, the mansion burned down under somewhat mysterious circumstances. The causes of the fire are unknown. Lady Pearl, however, seems to have been a resourceful and independent woman. Following the conflagration, she went to live with her sister-in-law, Emma Blamey, in St. John's. She was named sole executrix of the estate, and remained in St. John's for four years conducting its affairs. Anne was assisted in this work by John Lester, a farmer and native of Dorset, England.

In 1844, Anne left for England, but not before adding an additional 350 acres to her lands. She was fated never to roam her estate again, at least, not in her lifetime. Lady Pearl took up residence in London, and died there childless in 1860.

But Anne's story does not end there. Soon after her death, strange reports began to circulate around the farms and summer cottages near the Mount Pearl holdings.

As the legend is told, Anne's love of horse riding was stronger than the confines of the grave. Starting shortly after Lady Pearl's death, nocturnal visitors to her former riding grounds were witness to the figure of the lady, astride a phantom white horse.

Anne and her pale ghostly steed were seen on more than one occasion, although the circumstances of the sightings are today unclear.

Very little remains of the estate of Anne and James. The Admiralty House Museum sits in the midst of what was once Anne and James's oat field, and their racing grounds have vanished. Sadly, Anne herself has been quiet in recent years, resisting the lure of a midnight ride.

A GHOST NAMED PHIL
DUCKWORTH STREET, ST. JOHN'S

WHEN ONE THINKS OF GHOSTS, one might think of sinister spectres and terrifying apparitions. While Newfoundland certainly has its share of this type of ghost, it is also home to a phantom of a very different sort.

St. John's is well known for its colourful Second Empire-style row houses. One good example of this is the row of Victorian houses known as City Terrace on Duckworth Street, just west of what is now the CBC Radio building. City Terrace was the site of a fairly well-known murder case in the 1980s, and in light of that it might seem to be the perfect spot for a ghost of the most blood-curdling sort. One of the houses in the row, however, is in fact home to a most agreeable phantom.

The earliest resident of that house was Charles F. Stevenson, who was first recorded as living there in 1894. Charles worked as an accountant for the importer, general merchant, and political man-about-town, the Honourable George Knowling. Later in life, Charles shifted gears and worked as a commercial agent for A.W. Stevenson Ltd. in the wholesale provisions business. Under the auspices of A.W. Stevenson, Charles laboured as one of the

Newfoundland agents for Green Isle Blocks's "superior butterine," which was probably as "superior" as imitation butter could ever be.

By 1932, Charles Stevenson, overcome by oleomargine, had shuffled off this mortal coil. His widow shuffled off as well, but only as far as Colonial Street. After all the shuffling had settled, the house was occupied by a series of Baldwins, MacKinnons and Butts, and by the early 1990s the single-family home had been converted into separate apartments.

City Terrace, located in the centre of the photo immediately below the Star of the Sea Hall, is home to an amorous ghost nicknamed Phil. (Courtesy of the City of St. John's Archives)

It was about the time of the building's conversion to apartments that our friendly ghost began to make himself known. Over a number of years in the mid-nineties, the upper apartment was occupied by three women. In the years that they lived there, the trio shared the space with a ghostly inhabitant whom they nicknamed "Phil."

Phil, as far as ghosts go, seemed to be a spirit of a somewhat positive energy. Yet he chose, for the most part, to remain invisible. In fact, he revealed himself visually on only one occasion, close to the time of the women's arrival in the building. One of the women looked up one night while brushing her teeth to see a strange man standing at the top of the stairs. When she looked again the figure had vanished.

Phil made his presence known to the women through various tried-and-true ghostly tricks. These included hiding objects, turning on water taps, and walking around in the middle of the night. The odd door opening and closing by itself also hinted at something out of the ordinary in the apartment. In spite of these disturbances, the women never felt a sense of evil in the building. They also never felt threatened by the ghost, not even when one of them felt a man's hand resting on her shoulder one day as she was dressing.

Phil's friendliness, however, was best demonstrated through a rather unusual display of affection. Late one night, one of the women lay awake in bed, filled with a deep feeling of sadness and loneliness. Unable to sleep, she lay there alone in the darkness. Suddenly the door to the room opened slightly. Thinking that it was one of her housemates, the woman called out for whomever it was to come into the room.

The door opened of its own accord, hesitated for a moment, and then swung shut.

Next, the woman felt the nearness of another body in the bed beside her, an invisible figure that reached out and held her. In Phil's ghostly embrace, the woman was suddenly filled with a deep sense of comfort, and fell asleep almost immediately.

Who was this friendly phantom? Was it the ghost of one of the building's prior occupants, confused by the division of his former home into apartments? A lonely soul looking for love? Or was it the spirit of Charles Stevenson himself, doomed to wander eternity in search of quality dairy products? We shall probably never know.

PADDY MAHONY'S GOLD
LITTLE COLINET ISLAND, ST. MARY'S BAY

ONE OF NEWFOUNDLAND'S MORE INTRIGUING figures of the late nineteenth century was the Most Reverend Michael Francis Howley. When he wasn't busy acting as Archbishop, Howley found time to design the city's Coat of Arms, write countless letters to the English, Canadian and Newfoundland press, act as an authority on the controversy of Cabot's landfall, establish Mt. Cashel Orphanage, restore and beautify the Basilica, compose poetry and operettas, and design the Belvedere Orphanage building. He was something of a Renaissance man.

Howley also had a great interest in the folklore of Newfoundland. For ten years he contributed to the *Newfoundland Quarterly* a series of articles on the place names and legends of the Island. In December of 1909, Howley included in his regular *Newfoundland Quarterly* article a tantalizing story about a place called Horse's Head and an ill-fortuned man named Paddy Mahony.

Horse's Head was so named for a remarkable rock which had the appearance of, well, a horse's head. The rock is to be found on Little Colinet Island, which, together with its bigger brother Great Colinet Island, is situated in the middle of St. Mary's Bay.

While he was able to give a fairly certain explanation for the name of Horse's Head, the Most Reverend was less certain about the name "Colinet." Howley speculated that local people had derived this name from the word "colonel." Later researchers, however, argue that the name Colinet is both a French family name, and a place name, Collinette, in the Channel Islands.

Horse's Head was inhabited by the aforementioned Paddy Mahony, who dwelt in what Howley referred to as a "solitary hut." Somehow (and Howley is very vague on this point) it was revealed to the lucky Paddy that a great treasure was to be found in a certain place near Horse's Head.

Paddy lost no time, and set out with shovel in hand in search of the buried treasure. As the digging promised to be long lonely work, the recluse took his daughter with him for company. When Paddy reached the spot of the concealed loot, he sat the girl down on a rock where she could supervise his efforts.

Mr. Mahony set to work, digging as best he might. At last, it seemed that his exertions were to be rewarded. His shovel struck something hard, and upon further excavation, a great iron bound chest came into view.

No sooner had the top of the chest appeared at the bottom of the pit than Paddy heard a roar like thunder. This earth-shaking sound was quickly followed by a terrified scream from his distraught daughter.

Paddy looked up in time to see a raging bull rushing out from the bush and heading straight for his daughter on the rock. The bull charged, tail erect and horns lowered. Noble father that he was, Paddy forsook both the relative safety of the pit and the lure of the gold. Shovel raised, he charged the bull, ready to strike.

As Paddy ran for the bull, it suddenly vanished completely. When he returned to the pit, the chest had vanished as well.

When the man looked around, he saw at some distance from shore a small boat rowed by a solitary figure. The figure was described as a huge black man, and in the stern of the stranger's boat was a large iron bound chest.

The stranger rowed off into the distance and was never seen in St. Mary's Bay again. And what about our hero, the brave Paddy Mahony? Well, it seems he got neither the treasure, nor an explanation for the stranger's amazing transformation. Such is life.

SPIRIT CHILDREN
GOWER STREET, ST. JOHN'S AND
BRANCH, ST. MARY'S BAY

NESTLED AMIDST THE ROWS of Second Empire-style houses on Gower Street in St. John's is a building which is different from nearby houses for two reasons. First, it has a peaked gable roof where many of its neighbours have the curved mansard roofs so typical of much of the capital city's downtown. Secondly, it is the location of an unexplained paranormal sighting reported in 1996.

In July of that year a young woman was asked to look after the house while the owners were away. Normally not a superstitious person, the woman was seized by an indefinable dread while in the premises.

Because of this inexplicable feeling of terror while in the building, the young woman refused to spend a night alone in the house. Instead, she asked a close friend to stay over in the building with her. This second woman agreed and took a room in the back of the top floor of the house.

One night this friend awoke for no immediately explainable reason. There were no noises or disturbances which could have potentially awakened her. As she looked up, however, she saw a strange sight. There, standing between her bed and the window, was a figure she took for that of a teenaged boy.

The figure of the boy was silhouetted against the window, with a light shining in from outside. Because of the way the light fell, the strange boy's facial features could not be discerned. Peering at the figure, she could see that the boy had slightly protruding ears and what looked like closely cut hair. The boy stood silently for a moment, as if he were watching her. The figure then flickered, and was gone.

When the owners of the house returned, they claimed never to have seen such a figure, nor to have experienced the nameless dread the house-sitter had first felt. Intrigued, they investigated the history of the property with older people in the neighbourhood. This search revealed that no teenaged boy had ever dwelt there, only compounding the mystery of the event.

A similar sighting, that of an unknown child, was reported in June of 1998. This particular haunting was witnessed in the community of Branch. The visitation had occurred when the witness had been visiting a grandparent's house in the town.

As evening deepened, the person involved in the sighting decided to go to bed. After a while, they gradually started to fall asleep, but then suddenly felt a chill in the room. Opening their eyes, they could make out a shadow of what appeared to be a small child. A light had been left on in the room, and at first the eyewitness thought that something was blocking the light and casting the human-shaped shadow.

Looking closer, it became apparent that the "shadow" was not on the wall of the room. Instead, it actually had form and substance, and stood upright about a foot away from the wall. The area of darkness stood stock still for a moment, simply remaining suspended in space.

The frightened viewer watched the form in amazement; amazement which was replaced with horror when the head of the figure began to move, again like the thing was looking around the room. Scared beyond belief, the witness backed into the corner of the room and just stared at the spirit for approximately five minutes, too afraid to say or do anything, even after it vanished.

In both cases, the figures were never identified, and both sightings were only reported as happening once in each location. This type of haunting, the appearance of ghostly children, is perhaps due to the high rate of infant and child mortality in Newfoundland's past. Looking back into family histories, the death of children at a young age was a sadly common occurrence, and the family that did not suffer the loss of one of its younger members was a rarity.

The reasons for this high rate of child mortality varied, though part of it was due to the low level of professional medical care available two hundred years ago. The scarlet and putrid fevers, putrid sore throat, smallpox, and tuberculosis ensured that many a young Newfoundlander never made it to adulthood.

No community in the province was exempt to this regrettable reality. The loss of young family members to disease or accident is as much a part of the Island's history as any other tale. Perhaps the darkened figure in the bedroom was one of these tragic figures, tilting its head this way and that to search out someone, anyone, who would remember and retell the story of its short life.

THE SOIREE AT KELLIGREWS
CONCEPTION BAY SOUTH, CONCEPTION BAY

A NUMBER OF YEARS AGO, A MAINLAND MAN drove to the province on vacation with his family, and while here had experienced something which can only be described as unusual. While visiting Newfoundland, the family was driving through the community of Kelligrews. Realizing their car was getting low on gas, they stopped to fill up their tank at a local Ultramar gas station.

While the attendant was busily engaged in filling up the tank, the couple's four-year-old child mentioned what the man described as the "creepy-looking house across the street." Curiosity got the better of them, and when the tank was full, they drove over to have a look at the place.

When they drove by the front door, the father noticed that it was open, and therefore figured somebody was at home. He stopped the vehicle, walked up to the door and had a peek into the darkness inside. The house seemed abandoned, with no one visible in the interior.

Even more curious by this point, the father wanted to see what the porch was like, so he lit up his lighter. Looking around he caught sight of a small candle in the corner of the porch. The man went over to it, picked the candle up, and lit it. He then proceeded into the dim recesses of the building.

Just beyond the porch was the kitchen, followed by the hall. As he entered the hallway, the first thing he noticed was a picture of children who must have lived there long ago. As he looked at the picture, he was startled by a sudden noise above his head. He stood still and listened carefully. It sounded like children playing upstairs.

The man was half afraid to venture up the staircase because of its unsteady appearance. He heard the noise again. His immediate thought was that it was just a couple of local kids fooling around in the old building. Taking a chance he walked up the old stairs, to tell the children that they should not be playing in such an unsafe location, but when he reached the top storey there was not a soul to be found.

Mystified, he turned around to descend the stairs and found his exit blocked by a young boy. The boy pulled a face at the man, and then vanished into thin air right before his eyes.

Later, when the man told the story, all he could relate were his own personal experiences. To date the exact location of the haunting, if it was in fact such an event, has not been pinpointed. It remains nonetheless an interesting tale, particularly since the man knew little or nothing about the location, and was therefore not influenced by stories he had heard of the place. His experience remains one of Newfoundland's unexplained.

THE VANISHING CONDUCTOR
PORT UNION, TRINITY BAY

THE REID NEWFOUNDLAND RAILWAY played an important part in the development of this province. By 1915, several branch lines of the railway had been completed, including the line to Bonavista. In 1917 a spur railway from the Bonavista branch railway line was constructed from the Catalina station to the brand new Fishermen's Protective Union properties at Port Union. The Port Union Railway Station was built the same year.

If you travel to Port Union these days, you will see the local museum includes the original railway station. This beautiful little station has been relocated from a nearby wharf to its present location. Originally this station was the end of the line, the terminal stop on that branch of the railway. From Port Union, goods and passengers would switch from the rail cars to coastal boats to complete their journey.

Today the Reid Newfoundland Railway is long gone, indeed something of a ghost itself. However, it continues to be the source of many stories. Some of these are of a decidedly paranormal nature, and the Port Union station is involved in one of them.

During the later years of the Bonavista branch railway, after roads were constructed and bus services had been introduced, passenger-train traffic slowed down. As a result, by the late 1960s the trains ran on a reduced and fixed regular schedule, and did not generally run at night.

Late one night, in the fall of 1969, a man was travelling along the old Cabot Highway (currently Route 230) between Port Rexton and Port Union, just past Port Rexton in the Champneys/English Harbour area. As the man looked out over the bogs he saw a train. The man thought nothing of it, and travelled on until he got to the next railway crossing, when suddenly, and without warning, his car stalled just after he passed over the tracks.

Try as he might, the traveller could not get his car working. Then, out of the night, a man wearing a conductor's uniform and carrying a lantern came up to the car and asked for a ride into Port Union. Much like the driver of the car, he too was experiencing technical difficulties. The train had broken down unexpectedly, and the conductor needed to take word to the station in Port Union. The driver said that he would be glad to help, if only the car would start.

The driver tried his car again, and found that his vehicle, strangely enough, worked perfectly. The two men got in the car, and drove the distance from the crossing to Port Union. But when the driver arrived at the station and turned to see his passenger off, the conductor was no longer in the car! Presumably when the driver questioned the railway workers at the station, he was told there was no train running that night.

The mysterious conductor is very similar to what the American folklorist Jan Brunvand calls "The Vanishing Hitchhiker." This is a type of legend where the driver of a car turns to bid an unusual hitchhiker goodbye and discovers that the passenger has disappeared from the car. In many versions of the tale, the driver later learns that the mysterious passenger had died years before.

Sometimes the ghost leaves a book or scarf in the car, which grieving loved ones later identify as belonging to their long-lost husband, daughter, nephew or what have you. Unfortunately for us, the Port Union conductor left no such evidence of his ghostly ride. Many ghosts are said to be on endless quests, striving for peace and contentment in their earthly homes, returning to right a wrong done in life or to finish a task left incomplete. Whatever called the conductor back from beyond the grave may never be known.

Apparently, vanishing hitchhiker stories are told all over the world and date back over a hundred years, evolving from earlier European stories about travellers on horseback. As time rolled on, the wagons and horses of those days transformed, and by the time of the Great Depression, the evaporating spirit was riding the cars of today, or locomotives as the case may be.

Stories like this remind us that visitors from the spirit world can be encountered at any time and by anyone. The fact that the conductor could actually pass for a living person long enough to engage the driver in a conversation and enjoy a car ride only adds to the horror factor. Maybe you or I won't recognize a ghost the next time we meet one, either!

THE BATHING BEAUTY OF CLARKE'S BEACH
CLARKE'S BEACH, CONCEPTION BAY

LIKE MANY COMMUNITIES AROUND Conception Bay, Clarke's Beach is no stranger to the odd ghost story. The town of Clarke's Beach lies on the west side of Conception Bay, just a short drive south of Bay Roberts. The community first appeared in the census of 1857 with a population of 280. Many of its early settlers came from Bareneed and Port de Grave.

Unlike many of the other communities of Conception Bay, Clarke's Beach had no inshore fishery of its own. As a result, some of its inhabitants worked to prosecute the Labrador fishery, shipping out with merchants from Cupids, Brigus or Bay Roberts. After the 1880s, many of those who remained worked in the lumber industry, either working for Horwood Lumber or one of the other sawmills in the area, or making fish casks or drums.

Around 1984, three girls were out late one night, and were walking along the abandoned railway line that cuts through Clarke's Beach. The girls were walking from an area near Wilsonville Avenue along the track toward North River. Between North River and Clarke's Beach, the rail line runs over an old railway trestle, built when the line was in its heyday.

As the three girls drew closer, they could see a fourth girl sitting on the edge of the trestle, drying her hair with a towel, and drawing closer still they could see that the girl was dressed in an old- fashioned bathing suit. The bather paid no attention to the threesome, and it was not until they stepped onto the wooden beams of the trestle itself that the mysterious figure lowered her towel, and turned to look straight at them.

It was then that the threesome realized that something unnatural was afoot, and they stopped dead in their tracks. The figure of the girl gazed upon them, its eyes glowing with a brilliant red light, shining strong in the moonlight. The creature's malevolent gaze was enough to send the three tender young girls screaming in terror back to the relative safety of Clarke's Beach.

Later, the three learned that theirs was not the first sighting of the midnight bathing beauty, and in conversation with an elderly man who lived along Wilsonville Avenue, they also learned of the girl's tragic fate.

According to both the older gentleman and the folklore of the community, it seems that the form the three girls had sighted was the spectre of a local girl. This unfortunate young woman had died years before while swimming in the river beneath the trestle.

A mysterious bathing beauty with glowing eyes has been spotted on this trestle in Clarke's Beach, Conception Bay. (Courtesy of the Heritage Foundation of Newfoundland and Labrador)

As the story was told, the girl had arranged to meet her sweetheart for a late-night rendezvous and swim. After waiting and waiting, with no sign of her love, she took to the waters. Then, for reasons yet unknown, a dark tragedy ensued. The bathing beauty slipped beneath the silent waves and drowned alone in the darkness.

Apparently, the girl's ghost returned from the netherworld to haunt the spot of her demise, doomed to spend the sweet hereafter waiting by the railway line for a love that is fated never to arrive.

Today, the abandoned train trestle remains, even though the tracks themselves have long since vanished. The trains which once ran the tracks have disappeared, and their memory is becoming quickly ghostlike itself. The trestle still crosses the river, running parallel to the Conception Bay highway heading toward Bay Roberts. And the girl with the brilliant red eyes? Well, you'll have to wait for a moonlit night, and then cross the trestle yourself to find out.

PHANTOMS ON THE TRACKS
CORNER BROOK, HUMBER VALLEY

ONE OF CORNER BROOK'S GHOSTS is said to haunt the bed of the old railway track near Petries Street. Silent today, the railway first arrived in Corner Brook just over one hundred years ago, and for many years cutting ties for the railway was an important part of the work of Corner Brook's sawmills.

One summer night in late August, a young Corner Brook woman and her two male cousins were sitting in her aunt's backyard located just off Petries Street. From the yard, a person enjoying a conversation could look directly up the hill and see the train track. Very often, people would walk along the tracks on the way home, to work, or to visit a neighbour. Therefore, to hear the sound of feet coming up the track was not unusual.

On the night in question, one of the cousins was back-on to the track, while the other two people were facing it. As they chatted, the young woman looked up and was presented with a strange sight.

As she watched, she could see a woman dressed in a long white gown moving down the track. The gown itself was fairly unusual, but it was the manner in which the figure moved that caught the girl's attention. The female form possessed an unearthly fluidity in its movements. It was certainly not the sort of normal walking motion that you or I might use. Rather, it was a smooth, gliding motion, as if the woman's feet were not touching the ground at all.

The girl immediately pointed out the peculiar form to her two cousins. Both the boys could see the same figure. All three were in agreement that it was odd to see someone walking so smoothly on the track, and doubly odd that she should be attired in a long, flowing white dress.

Their curiosity aroused, the trio decided to walk up the hill to the track and investigate further. The track was only a stone's throw away. The three hurried to its edge to peer in the direction the women had headed. But when they got to the track, there was no sign of anyone in either direction, for as far as the eye could see.

Oddly enough, a ghostly woman has also been reported on the railroad tracks near Manuels, Conception Bay. On a fall evening a number of years ago, a sixteen-year-old left his grandmother's house to walk back home. The boy left the house and crossed the garden to the track at the rear of the property and began to walk the 150 feet or so on the crushed stone.

As he walked, he heard what he took to be another set of footsteps behind him. At first he thought it was just the sound of his own feet kicking up the crushed stones. When he realized that the steps were a distance behind him he turned around. What he saw terrified him.

The noise of the steps was still audible, but no one was making them. As he looked down toward the ground he watched the crushed stone being disturbed with the impressions of ghostly footsteps. Perhaps unsurprisingly, the boy ran the remaining distance.

The boy's sighting was not the first interaction with the ghost. According to the local oral tradition, a young woman by the name of Molloy had been killed on the track years before. Other sightings included the figure of a woman who was seen walking down a small path to the area, and a dark shadow which was reported blocking the entrance to the same path.

THE WHITE WOMAN
ARNOLD'S COVE, PLACENTIA BAY

PLACENTIA BAY HAS A FINE TRADITION of ghostly legends, and one of the most poetic comes from the community of Arnold's Cove. It incorporates three well-known, recurring themes in ghost lore: that of the lost lover, that of the lady in white, and that of the anniversary type of haunting where an event happens every year on the same date.

Sometime in the late 1800s, there were two young people who fell wildly in love. A wedding date was eventually scheduled for November 23. In a small community, a wedding was a cause for celebration, and all hands were excited.

The young man was, like most men in Arnold's Cove, a fisherman. He would often be gone for months at a time without anyone hearing from him. This particular year the young lover left in August but he promised his love that he would return in time for the wedding.

Months passed without any word of his whereabouts returning to the town. November arrived and plans for the wedding continued. But when November 20 and then the twenty-first came and passed, it was assumed by everyone in the town that he was not going to be back in time for the ceremony. The bride-to-be, however, had the utmost faith in her groom. She swore up and down that he would return in time to marry her.

The morning of the wedding day arrived, still with no groom. The girl remained sure he would be true to his word and began to prepare herself. She donned her dress and shoes, and just as she was adjusting her veil, she looked out the window.

There, sailing into the harbour, was the young man's ship. The community breathed a collective sigh of relief, and the girl sent her father down to the wharf to collect the groom and take him to the church.

She was almost ready to leave for the church when her father returned with tears in his eyes and grim news. The vessel had been caught in a storm and her promised one had drowned at sea.

At first the girl would not believe her father's words. She cried out that he would return, and that she would be married that day. She left her house, still wearing her wedding dress, and ran toward the harbour. From there she ran across the beach, through the woods, and toward a cliff overlooking the ocean.

The weeping bride stood there overlooking the cruel seas crying out the name of her beloved.

Finally, the poor maid realized he was fated never to return. In true melodramatic fashion, she flung herself off the cliff and plummeted to her tragic death.

The story, of course, does not end there. Not content to throw herself off the cliff once, our heroine returns every year, on the anniversary of her death, to the cliff where she met her untimely end. Or so goes the local folklore of Arnold's Cove.

Her ghost wanders the cliff, clad in her wedding dress and veil, weeping and wailing through the afterlife, pining away for her lost love. Known locally as "The White Woman," the tradition maintains that her ghostly self has been spotted by many and that her eldritch wailing has been heard by even more.

Very possibly, the story may be based on some real event which was passed down and embellished over the years. The only way to find out is to make a trip to Arnold's Cove next November 23.

THE KENNY'S POND CALLICANTZAROI

KENNY'S POND, ST. JOHN'S

O NE YEAR IN THE LATE 1970S, possibly 1977, and only a few days after the festivities of New Year's Eve, a St. John's man was out for an evening stroll. The man lived in the northeast end of St. John's, and was walking in the vicinity between Kenny's Pond and Mary Queen of Peace school.

There was not a full moon, but there was enough light in the sky to provide some illumination. There was no wind, and the little bit of snow which lay on the ground and on the branches of trees lent something of a picture-postcard look to the scene. The man walked on, enjoying the clean crispness of the winter air, until he came to a slightly barren area, surrounded by trees.

As he entered the clearing, the man's ordinary evening took an altogether extraordinary turn. There, waiting for him, was a very peculiar sight.

The walker saw what appeared to be the figure of a young person hunched on the ground. It crouched there, its thin arms wrapped around its knees, as if it were huddled for warmth. Warmth was clearly called for, as the figure wore absolutely no clothes.

There was a definite otherworldly quality to the being crouched in the fresh snow. The person seemed to be in his early teens, but it was hard to tell if it was male or female. The outline of ribs could be seen against the paleness of its chest, and white skin was stretched over the meagre frame of its skeleton, with bony knees and elbows jutting out sharply. It looked raw-boned, as if the creature had not eaten in some time.

If the hiker was shocked to see the strange apparition, it seemed as equally mystified to be discovered. It turned its face upwards in surprise, directing its gaze toward the man. Then, with a look almost of shame on its gaunt face, the creature unfolded its angular form and rose in the centre of the clearing. It stood, looked away, and then turned its back toward the astonished man, shoulder blades and angular hips almost protruding from parchment-like flesh.

Then, without warning, it vanished completely.

Twenty-five years later, there is no clear explanation of the identity of the strange being. If the man did actually see something in the clearing that wintery night, it could have been one of any number of different things. A ghost or phantom, perhaps, might be one explanation, but folkloric evidence suggests it may have been something more like one of the little people.

Certainly, there is a great tradition in the written and oral literature concerning the world of naked fairies. Brownies, a well-known type of forest spirit, are often reported as being naked and about three feet tall. However, they are usually brown, hence the name, with rumpled dark skin.

A much more similar type of little people to the Kenny's Pond creature is the Callicantzaroi. Not normally seen in Newfoundland, these are a type of strange thin fairies who are mostly witnessed as a group in Greece, Italy and Albania. According to researcher and writer Nancy Arrowsmith, "Callicantzaroi are the size of small children, skinny and always naked."

In addition to a similar physical appearance to the Kenny's Pond creature, the Callicantzaroi appear only during the Twelve Days of Christmas, and vanish from the world for another year on Old Christmas Day. This would tie in quite well with a sighting in the first few days of the New Year.

Regardless of whether the creature was a spirit apparition or a visiting Greek hobgoblin, the account remains one of the most eerie ever recorded from that portion of St. John's.

THE LADY OF LEWISPORTE
LEWISPORTE, BAY OF EXPLOITS

LEWISPORTE, LIKE MANY NEWFOUNDLAND communities, is no stranger to the occasional ghostly happening. One house in the community seems to be haunted by a fairly easygoing ghost. One night, one of the girls who lived in the house walked out of the bathroom to their mother's room to say good night to her. For no particular reason, she turned her head to look into her room. What she saw gave her a terrible fright.

The ghost of a late nineteenth century lady is said to haunt a house in the community of Lewisporte. (Courtesy of *Downhomer Magazine*)

The girl had gotten her bed ready for the night, but apparently a ghostly apparition was not satisfied with the way the sheets had been turned down. Much to her surprise, she saw what looked like two foggy hands of some sort, joined to a ghostly figure, pulling down the sheets a bit more, and smoothing the wrinkles out of the fabric.

One night while the same girl's stepfather was away working on the boats, the mother woke up to find the bed vibrating. Looking up, she saw a female figure standing in her closet. This woman looked to be in her early twenties, with dark hair pulled back in a bun. The ghost wore a dress which gave her the appearance of being from the late 1800s or early 1900s.

The mother stayed awake for a while and watched the woman. When the ghost did not move or make a sound, the mother simply fell asleep.

A while later, the same thing happened to the mother. She awoke from her slumber to find the same period-dressed woman looking at the jewellery on the bedroom dresser. The mother did not mind the phantom perusing her jewels, so she fell asleep again shortly afterwards.

THE GHOST IN SLIPPERS
GEORGESTOWN, ST. JOHN'S

ONE OF MY NEIGHBOURS CONTACTED ME after experiencing unusual activity in her family home. Her family did not feel threatened by these events, and indeed claimed to rather enjoy the playfulness of what she called "our spirit." The house itself is located on a well-known street in the Georgestown area of St. John's. The house is between eighty-five and ninety years old, but the property is much older, dating back to the mid-1840s.

Several of the spirit's antics appeared to be typical of ghosts everywhere. The family heard noises they could not explain, and electric lights flickered with no apparent cause. The playfulness of the ghost did not, however, prevent the woman from keeping holy water in the house, and crucifixes in most of the rooms.

The family's interaction with their ghost started on the day they took possession of the property. The husband was working abroad at the time, so it was just the mother and daughter living in the building. The mother was in the master bedroom on the upper storey, when she heard what seemed to be two or more women talking and laughing downstairs.

She remembers, "Thinking it was my mother and daughter, I called out to let them know where I was. When I received no reply, I went downstairs to look for them, but they were not there!"

Mystified, she looked around the house and found no one. She then ventured outside. Again, there was no sign of the women. Not thinking too much of it at the time, she shrugged off the event and returned to the house. She went upstairs to organize the bedrooms, and as she entered, the chandelier in the main bedroom started going on and off.

The woman recalls, "I admit I was a little spooked but again ignored it."

Later that winter the family had their first overnight guests. The mother's sister and her friend Mary arrived for a visit. It was the friend's first time in Newfoundland. After spending a night in one of the guest rooms, she announced that someone had called her at 9:00 A.M.

The ghostly visitor had called out to her, "Mary, it's nine o'clock, time to get up." Mary thought it was the sister calling, and went into the second guest room. She found the sister fast asleep, and there was no one else in the building who could have called her.

Since then, the family has also heard their names pronounced by phantom voices. The mother has, on several occasions, heard "Mommy" being called for. More recently, they have heard what seems to be a kind of shuffling noise upstairs. The noise, which generally occurs in the vicinity of the bedrooms, has been described as sounding like an elderly person scuffing about wearing slippers.

In addition to unusual noises, the strange forces at work in the building have caused solid objects to move around on their own. A large frying pan has flown off the stove on one occasion. Other objects have gone missing, only to be later found in unpredictable locations where no one would have sensibly put them.

JEREMIAH AND THE JERSEYMEN
BURGEO, SOUTH COAST

JEREMIAH WAS A BURGEO FISHERMAN. He got up in the dark early hours every morning and made ready to head out for a day on the water. One morning in the 1960s, Jeremiah woke and got ready to head out, just like many days before. He ate his breakfast and then got dressed in his oil skins. He pulled on his boots, left the house, and went down to the stage. The sun was just beginning to break over the horizon.

Just before the fisherman reached the stage head, he saw a frightening sight rise up from the rocks right in front of him. Three ghostly figures emerged directly out of the granite bedrock. Later, the man described them as looking like three ancient Jerseymen with weather-beaten faces. The three old men seemed to be talking in a foreign language, and arguing amongst themselves.

The appearance of the three weird figures had such an impact on Jeremiah that he had a slight heart attack. He fell to his knees on the ground, finding it hard to draw breath. Needless to say, he did not go out fishing that day, using the excuse that he was not feeling well. He never spoke of the sighting or of what he had experienced to his neighbours and friends, as he was afraid of being ridiculed by the local townspeople.

When he learned the story years later, the man's son was not so skeptical. "It makes sense to me because there was a crowd of Jerseymen that came to Burgeo in the late 1800s and early 1900s," remembers the son. "I'm not sure, though, if something tragic happened in that area of town or not."

Channel Islanders, particularly those from Jersey, began fishing in Newfoundland between 1600 and 1603. At that time Sir Walter Raleigh was Governor of Jersey, and it is said he encouraged them to become involved in the Newfoundland fishery.

Jersey merchants had arrived in Burgeo as early as 1840, if not before. The first European settlers to Burgeo arrived in the late 1700s, and by 1802 it had a booming population of twenty-three. In 1840, the noted Jersey firm Nicolle and Company set up shop in the community. The Channel Island company had established a base in Newfoundland circa 1789, and was one of the first major mercantile operations in Fortune Bay.

The family firm ceased trading in 1863. One of the early principals of the company, Philippe Nicolle, Sr. (1769-1835), had built a large house in Jersey with the proceeds of the Newfoundland fish trade. Nicolle's house was turned into a museum in 1893. It is still operated as such, and is open to tourists visiting the Channel Islands.

The people of Jersey themselves believe they were in Newfoundland much earlier than 1600. One old tradition holds that a group of Jersey fishermen, on their way to Iceland, were driven off course by storms. They were pushed to the southwest until they reached a land surrounded by waters teeming with fish. Some Jerseymen believe that John Cabot learned of the rich fishing grounds from them, and that his discovery was based on something the people of the Channel Islands were well familiar with.

Much like Newfoundlanders, the people of Jersey have a rich tradition of folklore, and the Island boasts many stories of witches, strange creatures, ghostly carriages, black dogs and phantoms of all types. Three Jersey ghosts would doubtlessly feel quite at home on our own haunted shores.

CHAPTER 3

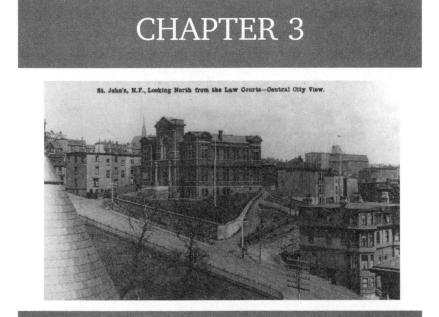

St. John's, N.F., Looking North from the Law Courts—Central City View.

Tokens, Premonitions, and Guiding Lights

DEATH TOKENS

LIVINGSTONE STREET, ST. JOHN'S

ONE OF THE MOST COMMON TYPES of hauntings reported in Newfoundland is that of the "token" or "death token." A death token is where a person becomes aware, through some paranormal means, that a person close to him has recently died. The victim may appear visually to the bereaved, or the loss may be communicated in some other fashion, such as through the stoppage of a clock or some unexplainable event. Tokens have taken the form of animal figures, strange noises, moving lights, and voices calling as if from a great distance.

A very typical ghostly token was witnessed over a relatively short period of time in the 1960s. A younger male relative of the woman, who lived in 9 Livingstone Street in downtown St. John's, had vanished under somewhat mysterious circumstances. Following his disappearance, his translucent form appeared to the woman.

The apparition would materialize to hover at the foot of her bed in her bedroom on the upper storey, and appeared before her each and every night until his body was found at the bottom of Signal Hill. Murder was whispered about, but nothing conclusive ever came of the case. From that point to this, his ghost has not been witnessed since.

The appearance of a token may also be taken to mean that someone's death is about to occur. Many things have been interpreted as signs, omens or tokens of a coming death. These have included strange rapping noises on the side of a house, or the sudden stoppage of a clock. Some tokens of death are a little more unusual. Around 1900, the people of Bay Roberts believed that a hollow square resembling a coffin, seen in a boiled pudding, signified death. It is almost enough to make you think twice about what you might serve for Sunday dinner!

THE SPENCER SPIRIT
PORT AUX BASQUES, SOUTH COAST

LIKE MANY A NEWFOUNDLANDER living either in the province or outside it, Tina Spencer is no stranger to those unexplained happenings that make us question the nature of life and death. Nor is she a stranger to the power of love, and the ability of love to transcend the boundary between this world and the next.

Spencer currently lives in Berwick, Nova Scotia, where she has lived with her mother since 1988. She was born in Port-Aux-Basques in August 1973 to David and Mabel Spencer, and as a babe was the apple of her father's eye.

Though still a young man, David Spencer became convinced that he would not live to see thirty years of age. When Tina was still very young, he grew sick, and as his illness deepened, he grew more and more concerned about his daughter's life and future. Eventually, the man was sent to hospital. While there, he asked his wife to make him a number of promises about his daughter.

At the time, his wife thought it was foolish, but seeing that he was so convinced that he would not recover, she agreed to do what she could. His final wish was that Tina would graduate school. Sadly, time proved the man's fears justified, and he passed away at age twenty-seven of heart failure. His daughter Tina was only three.

Time passed, and it became obvious that while David Spencer had left this world behind in body, his spirit remained to look over his family. On the morning of his young widow's thirtieth birthday, she awoke to see her late husband and his father, also deceased, standing by her bed. The ghost of her husband wished her a happy birthday, and then just faded away. As Tina Spencer relates, "My mom was a long time getting over that, and to this day she still talks of it."

In 1991, Tina was in grade twelve and it looked like she would not graduate. The girl was tempted to quit school but her mother, remembering her husband's final wish, refused to accept that as a possibility. She implored the girl to get extra help. Ultimately the mother's desire to see her succeed was fulfilled, and her wish to keep her promise was granted. Tina did in fact graduate.

On the eve of the young woman's graduation she had a very restless night. She remembers, "I kept hearing footsteps coming down the hall and in my room. Then I would feel like someone was in my room. I would see the bed move and see an imprint like someone was sitting on the bed by my side."

The girl was terrified, but as her fear grew, the invisible guest seemed to leave. She heard the footsteps retreat up the hall. As she grew calm once more, the eerie happenings repeated. Scared once more, she called out for her stepsister Heather to join her. At first, the second girl thought Tina was being foolish. Before long, however, the ghostly visitor made its presence known once more, leaving both girls very afraid.

The girls' mother was out of town that evening, but returned the next morning in time for the graduation ceremony. She sat with the girls, who related their strange experiences of the night before.

As the three talked over the events, they began to wonder if the figure might not have been that of the father, watching over the girl. As his last wish had been for the girl to graduate, they thought perhaps that it had been he who came back on the eve of the ceremony. Perhaps it was he who was the ghostly figure sitting on the bed, and he who was responsible for the footsteps in the hallway.

THE MISSING BODY
FOGO, FOGO ISLAND

Business left unfinished may cause a ghost to appear. Sometimes a ghost will appear to reveal the location of a will or money, or to bid farewell to someone they had not been able to speak with before their death. In a ghost story from Fogo, first recorded in 1978, a ghost appeared to pinpoint the location of his own missing corpse.

The story tells of a young man from Fogo about twenty-five years old at the time of his tragic death. "Harry" was a personable fellow and was well liked by everyone who lived in the settlement. Therefore, it was a great tragedy for the community that he drowned in the cove not far from his home, leaving behind him a grieving young wife and family and friends shocked by their loss.

Another part of the tragedy was the fact that Harry's body could not be found following the drowning. Such was the feeling of community solidarity that every man in the harbour turned out to help search for Harry's body.

It was widely guessed that the body was located somewhere in the shallow cove. The men set to work to find the location of the body, so that they could then drag it up and give it a proper Christian burial.

The crew tried for a week to find the missing corpse, but try as they might, they could not find it.

Some people in the search party expressed their doubt that the body would ever be found at all. They believed that the natural ebb and flow of the tide had taken the corpse of poor Harry out to sea.

As days went by, their fears grew deeper. After eight days, hopes of finding the body of the drowned man dwindled. After the eighth day of searching, the sorrowful search party returned to shore. Another long, fruitless day of dragging was left behind them, with no body brought back for burial.

One of the younger men in the party tied up his punt and started for home. The young man had been a close friend of the missing man, and was as tormented by the loss as if it had been his brother. As he neared his house, he was greeting by a strange apparition. Standing by the side of the road, looking very real, was the figure of Harry. He looked almost the same as he had in life, except for the fact he was ghostly pale, and that long strands of seaweed were twisted into his hair and hanging from his clothes.

The ghost of Harry then opened his mouth and spoke to the young man. The ghost told his friend not to be afraid, and announced that he had appeared to reveal the exact location of his corpse. The spirit informed the amazed man that his body could be found lying in less than six feet of water, wedged under a rock near a particular stage head. Having delivered the coordinates of his corpse, the ghost then evaporated into the evening air.

The next morning the young man told the rest of the search party of his eerie experience. They made for the stage head. After a few minutes of jigging the rock, the body was revealed and brought to the surface. Harry was brought to shore, and was given a decent burial. This apparently appeased the spirit of the man. From that point on he rested quietly in the graveyard, and the good people of Fogo never saw his phantom again.

THE WAR BRIDE
FORT PEPPERELL, ST. JOHN'S

ACCORDING TO THE OLD RECORDS of the Canadian Department of National Defence, the years between 1942 and 1948 saw over 64,000 war brides and their dependants immigrate to Canada. All told, nearly 45,000 British and European women left behind everything that was familiar to start a new life on this side of the ocean.

The adventures of the war brides who settled here are filled with love, passion, tragedy and joy. One Newfoundland example is somewhat different from these. True, it encompasses all these emotions, but it also features a decidedly paranormal twist.

A story is told of a St. John's man who had joined the Merchant Navy in 1940. While overseas the Newfoundlander met a beautiful Scottish girl, and they fell in love. It was decided that the two should marry. Together they made plans that when the war was over she would return with him to Newfoundland, like so many other war brides.

Unlike the thousands of others who found happiness on these shores, once the woman came to Newfoundland she found it not to her liking. Eventually the lass decided to return to her native home in Scotland. The man, distraught, pleaded with her in a series of letters to come back. The woman refused. She wrote back, saying that as much as she loved him, she could not leave the Scottish hills where she was born.

Time passed, and with the distance between them, the man began to forget the woman he had married, the memory of his Scottish love beginning to fade like the mists on the moors. Eventually, his wartime passions having cooled, he began going around with a St. John's girl.

It was at this point that an odd thing happened. Following the war, the man had found employment at Fort Pepperell. Much to his surprise one day as he checked out of the guard room, he found the Scottish lass waiting for him on the sidewalk.

"I am very sick at home," she said, "and I was thinking of you so much I just had to see you."

As soon as she had spoken these words, the woman's form began to dissipate, and she faded away into thin air. The man had never experienced such a thing, and his response was intense. He

A man working at Fort Pepperell, shown here in the 1940s, was visited by the spirit of his Scottish war bride. (Courtesy of the City of St. John's Archives)

was so affected by the sudden appearance and subsequent ethereal dematerialization of the female form that passersby rushed to his aid, thinking he had suffered a heart attack.

When the man had recovered, he at once sent a cable to Scotland. The reply came the next day, and it advised him that his wife was dying. It was believed that the end was nigh. He cabled back with the news that he would fly to Scotland immediately.

The man then hurried to the airline office to purchase a ticket for the flight. According to one source, the airline office at that time was located quite close to the old Newfoundland Hotel. He bought the ticket, and as he stepped out of the office, his wife again was standing there to greet him.

The vision spoke to him a second time, but this time her news was even more chilling. The form told him that she had died that very morning, and that she had come to him to say goodbye before returning to the Scottish hills. Once again she turned to mist and faded away.

The man dropped to the sidewalk, rendered unconscious from the shock of the event. It was while recuperating in hospital that the man learned officially that his wife had died that very day.

THE STRANGE CASE OF MRS. DOWER
CONCHE, GREAT NORTHERN PENINSULA

THE BELIEF THAT THE SPIRIT of a loved one would appear at the moment of death was not uncommon throughout Newfoundland's history, even into the present day. Sometimes, in special circumstances, powerful emotions even had the power to blur the line between life and death altogether. An example of this can be found in the strange tale of Mrs. Ellen Dower of Conche.

On March 10, 1872, Skipper Edward Dower left Conche with his son on board his ship the *Elsie* to prosecute the lucrative seal fishery. Mrs. Dower, who loved her husband very much, became ill a week after he had left, and within a matter of hours, died, much to the shock of the community. During the second night of the wake for poor Mrs. Dower, the *Elsie* slipped back into port, its flag at half mast. No sooner had the ship entered the port than a truly miraculous event occurred.

Much to the terror of the mourners keeping vigil beside her, the dead woman emitted a great sigh, and suddenly sat straight up in her coffin. The corpse then spoke, saying, "I am tired. I have been far. I have been with Ned."

While this may sound unbelievable, apparently she had. When Skipper Ned Dower reached his house, he told the assembled crowd that the ghost of his wife had appeared to him while on the ice. Convinced that he had seen a token of her death, he put his flag at half-mast and returned home with his son to attend the funeral. The spirit of his wife, it seems, had followed his ship out to the ice while her body remained at home, such was her love and anxiety for his safety. The good captain, it is said, never went to the ice again.

THE PHANTOM AND THE OPERA
PETTY HARBOUR, AVALON PENINSULA

Quite often, ghost stories involve a spirit who comes back to complete unfinished business or to simply bid a fond farewell to one loved dearly in life. One such story is told about a woman from Petty Harbour who passed away about 1985. She returned from the great beyond in an unusual way to say goodbye to one of her grandnephews.

The haunting took place when the nephew was in his early teens, about fourteen or fifteen years of age. His father's sister was a bit of a character. The woman was fun-loving, loud, and boisterous, but she was regarded by some as the black sheep of the family due to one peculiar trait.

While the woman was part of a very traditional Newfoundland fishing family content with the usual musical fare, the aunt, for her part, dearly loved opera. She would listen to opera on CBC Radio all the time, tuning in every chance she got to La Boheme and the Barber of Seville.

Every good story, as true opera fans will attest, involves a death, and the tale of the Petty Harbour woman is no exception. But instead of being stabbed to death by a jealous lover, she died of natural causes one night in her sleep. She had been in her early eighties, and was buried in Petty Harbour.

One of her grandnephews, an aspiring playwright and actor, felt that he was heir apparent to the old woman's reputation of being the black sheep of the family. From the day she died, that boy experienced a rather strange series of events.

The family had a modern portable stereo. It was one of the first of its kind, with electronic programmed channels, as opposed to the old manual kind with the push buttons where you would hear the mechanism move from one channel to the next. All you had to do was barely touch the button, and it would move to the next channel.

The stereo had been commandeered by the boys of the family, and as a result was programmed to the local Top Forties and rock stations. Needless to say, CBC Radio was not one of the channels that were programmed. Yet, whenever the nephew was in the house alone, the stereo would come on by itself. Even more curiously, it would be tuned to CBC Radio and would be playing opera.

The first time it happened, the nephew pushed the button to change the channels, and found that the stereo simply would not change from station to station. He then tried pushing the on/off button, but it would not shut off. As he discovered, the only way he could get it to stop at all was to completely unplug the machine from the wall.

The strange event then repeated itself when he was home alone again. Needless to say, he began to find the bizarre behaviour of the stereo somewhat disturbing. He told a friend about it and she laughed, thinking he was making it up. He told his family, who were equally skeptical. At first the boy thought it was an electronic problem, but as the weeks passed he became more intrigued and wondered if there were more paranormal causes.

Two weeks after the great-aunt had died, the disturbances simply stopped. After that, the stereo worked perfectly, and there were never problems again with the on/off switch. To this day, the nephew likes to think it was the other black sheep of the family saying goodbye in her own characteristically unique way.

THOMAS NEWMAN'S PREMONITION
LONDON, ENGLAND

———

On July 15 of the year 1815, Napoleon Bonaparte was received on board the HMS *Bellerophon*. Napoleon, banished from Europe as a disturber of the peace, had surrendered himself to the English Navy, and the *Bellerophon* had been sent to carry the former general and emperor to his exile in St. Helena.

According to local folklore celebrated each year with a toast to the Queen at the Newman Wine Vaults Provincial Historic Site, Napoleon's surrender had an important Newfoundland connection.

Earlier, in March of that year, the HMS *Bellerophon* had been stationed in Newfoundland, and a hogshead of Newman's Celebrated port had been purchased, for the use of the officers, from the Newman's agent, one Mr. Teage.

The surrender of Napoleon was toasted by the officers of the *Bellerophon*, possibly with the port wine which had aged in the old stone vaults on Water Street, St. John's. The vessel's logbook, now in the possession of the London Record Office, records that in their patriotic zeal the officers drained eighty-eight gallons of wine to commemorate the occasion.

A Newman and Company ship, much like the barquentine Retriever *shown here in Harbour Breton, was lost after a strange premonition.* (Courtesy of Newfoundland Historic Trust)

Today, the Newman Wine Vaults are preserved as one of the oldest buildings in the West End of St. John's. The stone-lined vaults themselves would seem to be an ideal spot for a ghost story. Yet they seem to be free of anything even remotely paranormal, and are only haunted by memories of spirits of a thoroughly drinkable kind.

This is not to say that Newman and Company is not associated with the odd eerie tale. The Newmans were established in Newfoundland as early as 1589, and with a history dating back over four hundred years, the Newmans were no strangers to Newfoundland's unexplained.

One such story involved one of the firm's sailing vessels, the *Talbot*. In 1892, the year of the St. John's Great Fire, the *Talbot* slipped its moorings in Oporto, Portugal, and sailed out on the tide, bound for Newfoundland. The ship was under the command of Captain Putt, a native of Salcome, Devon, not far from the Newmans' ancestral home of Dartmouth.

At that time, the firm of Newman and Company was under the direction of senior partner Mr. Thomas Holdsworth Newman (1825-1894). Thomas Holdsworth Newman was the third son of Sir Robert William Newman (1776-1848), the first Baronet and Member of Parliament for Exeter. It was under Thomas Holdsworth Newman's direction that the firm of Baine, Johnston and Company was made the agent for Newman's Port, an appointment the firm still holds over a hundred years later.

Thomas's foresight and good business sense in choosing Baine, Johnston and Company as his agent is not remarkable when viewed in light of the fact that he had a proven track record of precognition.

As Captain Putt and the crew of the *Talbot* sailed across the turbulent waters of the North Atlantic, Thomas was safely on land back in England. One night, he had a disturbing premonition in a dream. In the vision, Thomas foresaw an impending disaster that would strike the vessel. The director woke with start, and realized with horror that he had not insured the vessel.

In the morning Thomas made haste to the offices of his insurance agent, and insured the *Talbot* and its cargo for its full value. Apparently, the warning in the dream had materialized in the nick of time. Mysteriously, the *Talbot*, Captain Putt and his crew, along with a full cargo of Newman's finest port, vanished into the sea. Not so much as a timber of the vessel was ever seen again.

THE LIGHTS OF GALE'S ISLAND
GRAND CODROY RIVER
CODROY VALLEY

M YSTERIOUS LIGHTS HAVE A GREAT tradition of their own here in the province. There are numerous stories from around Newfoundland and Labrador of an eerie light that would appear in times of danger and was usually followed by a tragic incident.

This pale flame, known in Latin as ignis fatuus, has been oft-times reported flickering over marshy ground, and, it is said, over churchyards. It often appears specifically to lead travellers astray, into bog holes, or over cliffs.

For many, the ignis fatuus is a type of fairy or possibly ghostly spirit found all over the British Isles and Newfoundland. In the United Kingdom the phenomenon is known variously as a hinky-punk, a hobby-lanter, or a Joan-in-the-wad. Another English name was the Jill-burnt-tail, said to be a more flirtatious, female version! It was known as the ellyll-dan in Wales, but is most famously known by its Irish name, the will-o'-the-wisp. In fact, a quick Internet search revealed over three thousand Web sites containing references to the will-o'-the-wisp!

This strange phenomenon is known most commonly in Newfoundland as the jacky lantern, the West Country England name for the will-o'-the-wisp. However, it was also known as a corpse light in the Harbour Grace area, and as a corpse candle around St. John's.

No entirely satisfactory explanation has been put forward to explain the origin of these strange lights, but that has not stopped people from trying. A colourful Newfoundland folk tale relates that the will-o'-the-wisp is named after an Irish blacksmith named Will who outsmarted the Devil. Being too bad for Heaven, and with the Devil unwilling to let him into Hell, Will was doomed to wander for all time, with only a burning wisp of paper to guide his way through the darkness.

It is generally believed in scientific circles that the effect is due to the spontaneous combustion of gases, especially methane or phosphine. This gas would be produced by the disintegration of dead plant or animal material, typical for the boggy terrain where the lights are seen.

Other skeptics have argued that tectonic strain in rocks, in particular those near active fault lines, can cause strange light phenomena. Unusual "tadpole-shaped" lights were seen before an earthquake in Leicestershire in February 1957, and jacky-lantern type lights appeared before an earthquake in Cornwall in November 1996. In his 1982 book *Earthlights*, author Paul Devereux argued that some of these phenomena can be recreated under laboratory conditions.

Ghost orbs and glowing circles of white light are becoming the most widely reported types of hauntings in the world. Internet Web sites with literally thousands of photographs of these orbs are popping up like mushrooms in the night of cyberspace. Skeptics and experts hotly debate the authenticity of the balls of light, blaming them on magnified dust motes, droplets of water, electrical emissions, and normal geologic processes. Ghost hunters and believers argue that they may be some type of mobile, sentient energy that can change its appearance and location at will, like the jacky lanterns or will-o'-the-wisps of Newfoundland folklore.

I personally have yet to see such a moving light. But if I should happen to have that opportunity, I certainly hope it is the flirtatious Jill-burnt-tail, and not the product of something as mundane as shifting tectonic plates.

There are numerous stories from all across the province of eerie lights, and equally as numerous explanations for their causes. The Codroy Valley on the Island's west coast is one area that is no stranger to these unearthly illuminations.

Starting in the 1840s, a large number of Scots from Cape Breton settled in the Valley, and brought with them the customs and traditions of Cape Breton and their Scottish homeland. One example of these ghost lights is to be found in Margaret Bennett's book *The Last Stronghold*, which deals with the Scottish Gaelic traditions of the region.

On the north bank of the Grand Codroy River is a spot known as Gale's Island. Local tradition holds that the first settler of the Valley was a man named Gale who arrived in the 1770s with an English crew of shipbuilders. When the crew left for England in the fall, Gale opted to remain in Newfoundland. A gravestone located near the Grand Codroy River is dated 1815 and bears the name of John Gale. Whether named for Mr. Gale or not, Gale's Island was the focal point for strange pyrotechnics for a number of years. In fact, it was said that the lights were seen, on and off, for around twenty-five years.

The ghost lights always followed the same routine. A ball of light would appear, and would hover close to the ground for some time. After it had remained there for a while, it would start to rise into the air. The light would rise up about twenty feet, would then burst, shimmer, and change colour to red.

After this display was complete the light would return to ground level and start over once more. The light would start to rise up again, getting brighter as it rose, but never changing size.

Margaret Bennett's informant told her that people in the area were so used to the strange happening that they paid it no mind at all. The display was seen in the same place for many years, and then vanished. It was not seen again.

THE BLUE LIGHT SPECIAL
LEWISPORTE, BAY OF EXPLOITS

DURING THE FIRST WEEK IN AUGUST of either 1997 or 1998, a Lewisporte woman experienced a very odd thing. One morning, at 3:00 A.M., a brilliant bright blue light woke her from her sleep. She woke to find that the entire bedroom had turned completely blue.

A strange blue glow was reported over the community of Lewisporte in the late 1990s. (Courtesy of *Downhomer Magazine*)

The light lasted about one minute. As the woman sat there in bed, the light disappeared very suddenly.

Naturally curious as to the cause of the blue light, she immediately got out of bed to look out the window. All the street lights had gone out as far as the eye could see, pitching the whole town into an inky darkness.

The next morning the woman spoke to her sister about the event. The sister lived one mile away, and she claimed to have been awake when a brilliant blue light had filled her bedroom. The sister looked out her window to see the trees, the sky, the houses, indeed, everything in sight, shining a brilliant blue colour. The glow suddenly disappeared and everything went black.

The sisters never found an explanation for the blue light.

THE BAR LIGHT
RANDOM ISLAND, TRINITY BAY

I MADE MY FIRST TRIP TO RANDOM ISLAND seven years ago in the tow of my then new girlfriend, Kelly Jones. She took me to the community of Britannia to meet her grandmother, Lucy Leawood. Mrs. Leawood was a spry, charming woman, a renowned cook, and avid gardener. She welcomed me into her house, made sure I was fed, and treated me to the hospitality for which Newfoundlanders are rightfully famous.

Random Island is one of Newfoundland and Labrador's great treasures and one of the most beautiful spots in the province. Although it is indeed an island, Random Island cannot be circumnavigated except by small boats. This is due to the fact that normal passage around the island is blocked by a shoal. The sandy shoal runs off Random Island's northwest corner and marks the division between two sounds; Smith Sound on the north side, and the Northwest Arm of Random Sound on the south side.

Locally, this spit of land is known as "The Bar." In 1952, the Hefferton Causeway was built across The Bar, connecting Random Island to the "mainland" portion of the province. Like everyone these days who visits Random Island by car, I too crossed the causeway on my way to meet Nan Leawood and her family.

Over the years, The Bar has attracted a number of stories. One of the more intriguing stories is about a mysterious phenomenon named The Bar Light, and I am indebted to Geoff Adams for bringing it to my attention.

Although he now lives in Vancouver, Geoff Adams grew up in the area, on the mainland side of The Bar. The location was long regarded as a good site for logging. In the 1760s, Benjamin Lester noted in his diaries that families from Trinity used that part of Smith Sound as a site for winter logging operations.

Geoff Adams's family has a long connection to the region. William Adams began winter work there in 1867. He liked the site so much, he moved his family there in the fall of 1869 as the first permanent settlers. Later generations of Adamses built up lumbering as the primary industry, rafting logs in booms up the Sound. According to the *Encyclopedia of Newfoundland and Labrador*, tradition maintains that while most of the lumber was used for home and schooner construction, in later years a large quantity of it was used in the making of biscuit boxes for Purity Factories.

Many inhabitants of the area claim to have seen the local phenomenon known as The Bar Light, including Adams's own father. According to reports, the appearance of the light follows the same general description each time it is witnessed. As Adams's uncle told him, "on certain nights, usually from spring to autumn, a ball of light can be seen bobbing up over the water from the farthest reaches of Smith Sound."

The light starts from the area around the community of Harcourt, and then slowly makes its way up the Sound, heading toward the Hefferton Causeway. The glow hovers just above the water, dancing over the waves, heading toward Clarenville, until it reaches the sand spit. Once it reaches this point, it disappears suddenly.

Legend has it that the light is that of the kerosene lamp which belonged to a party of four young people. The party was made up of two men and two women. Adams relates, "One of the men is supposed to be a distant relative of mine on my mother's side, from Shoal Harbour."

The people involved were Mr. and Mrs. Hogarth, Mr. William Wiseman (Adams's maternal relative) and Mrs. Mary Ann Leonard from Shoal Harbour. They had walked to Snooks Harbour on the ice, and the foursome was returning home, sometime in the late hours of a winter night in the 1870s. They were headed home from a church gathering, walking over the ice.

One of the men held a lantern in one hand, guiding the way to safety. The crisp winter wind blew around them and they pulled their coats tighter to their bodies. Perhaps one of the men extended a protecting arm around his loved one's shoulders, drawing her closer. Perhaps one of the women thought of her family at home, and the warmth of the kitchen fire waiting there.

As they walked on, the doomed couples were unaware of sinister forces at work beneath them. Undercurrents at play around the sand of The Bar had undermined their walking surface, wearing away the ice to a dangerous and deadly thinness.

As they drew closer to The Bar, the ice gave way without warning. With a cry, with a shout, with a desperate grasp at the fragmented ice, with a sense of absolute despair, all four sank beneath the bitterly cold waters of the Sound. The kerosene lantern sank like a stone, its pale flame guttering and extinguishing in the wet darkness.

A man by the name of Eli Stanley from George's Brook was walking along the shore toward Shoal Harbour. He heard the screams and for a moment saw Mrs. Hogarth, but she soon vanished. Shocked, he hurried to Shoal Harbour for help, but it was too dark and too late to be of any use. The next morning, a group returned with ice- and pit saws to retrieve the bodies.

There is no marker along the Causeway to Random Island commemorating the spot where they vanished beneath the ice. The only memorial to their passing is a strange light seen on certain nights between spring and fall. The light moves, bobbing along just above the surface of the water, like a lost soul desperately trying to find its way back to solid ground.

Early in 2003, I made my way across the Causeway on my most recent visit to Random Island. It was a cold and windy winter's day, one probably similar to that day many years before. I returned to Random Island on that day for the funeral of Lucy Leawood. On that day, it was those gathered together in Britannia's wooden church that were the lost souls whose firm path had vanished beneath their feet.

However, I find it hard to believe that the shining light that was Mrs. Leawood will ever truly be extinguished. She will always be a part of Random Island, both for me, whose life she touched so briefly, and for her family and friends whose loss is so much greater. Her memory will always be that burning lantern, guiding those she left behind through the darkness, helping them find their way back to solid ground.

FOOTSTEPS AND ORBS
ROCKY HARBOUR, BONNE BAY

WHEN MANY PEOPLE THINK OF hauntings they think of old ghost stories involving headless pirates, guarding their buried booty, or Victorian ladies in white gowns drifting through the night. For these people, hauntings happened a hundred years ago, and are seen as old tales passed down by storytellers and black-cloaked tour guides.

Yet while there are dozens of tales of ancient spirits in the province, hauntings continue to occur up to the present day. A good example is a recent series of paranormal events which took place in December 2001 in Rocky Harbour on the west coast of Newfoundland.

Rocky Harbour is an old community with a rich history. Local lore tells of a murder there in 1809. A trapper from St. Margaret's Bay, named John Pelley, worked an area around Cow Head during the winter. The man murdered Richard Cross and Joseph Rendell when they trespassed on his trapping territory. He was later tried and executed by hanging in St. John's.

The haunting in question, however, is not one linked to events past or historical figures. Instead, the events took place in a fairly modern house built by its current occupants. The occurrences ranged from visual sightings and auditory experiences to electrical disturbances.

The first indication that something was wrong was an electrical disturbance witnessed by the father of the family. The gentleman was sitting on the couch watching television, when the set shut off by itself. Suspicious that a nearby family member with the remote had turned it off, he looked for the culprit. The nearest person was in the next room, ignorant of the set's contrariness.

That simple event was the first of what would become a trinity of mysterious happenings. The second event took place one morning at about 10:00 A.M. A late-sleeping son woke to hear footsteps in the hallway. At first, he took them for his mother's. The footsteps were quite rapid and were moving back and forth along the passageway. As the son sat up in his bed, the sound of the footsteps came into the bedroom, past the foot of the bed, and then alongside of the bed where he was sitting. The footsteps then ceased. Not once were the feet responsible for the clamour visually revealed.

The third event was the most dramatic. The same son was watching television in the bedroom one night when he caught a glimpse of a reflection in the dresser. He looked up to see strange white light. The son described the light as an "orb" which then began to rotate. The glowing orb of light spun around three times, hovering well off the floor. The placement and movement of the orb ruled out the hypothesis that it was a reflection from the television screen.

The son theorized that the occurrences might be linked to the spirit of his grandfather, a man who died farther up along the coast before the son's birth. Whether it is due to a grandfatherly spirit or natural subterranean forces, the cause of the Rocky Harbour haunting and its glowing orb remains unexplained.

FROM GHOST LIGHTS TO UFOS
CODROY VALLEY

As we as a society become more technologically focussed, the old explanations for strange lights in the sky, dancing over valleys, or leading berry pickers astray, have changed. It would seem, to some extent, that the ghostly rays of light and the corpse candles of yesteryear have transformed into unidentified flying objects and flying saucers.

In 1986, British author Phil Reeder argued that accounts of the jacky lantern were common in popular and scientific literature toward the end of the nineteenth century. However, these reports have decreased at the same time as reports of UFOs have increased. This seems to be the case for the Codroy Valley. Strange lights continue to be seen, but the explanation now is that they are alien spacecraft.

One evening in July of 1984, a group of friends were playing softball. One of the ballplayers happened to look over his shoulder. As he did so, he caught sight of something very odd. There, over the hill behind him, he saw two dark gray objects cutting through the evening sky.

The man immediately realized that these strange objects were definitely not aircraft or shooting stars, nor were they caused by atmospheric conditions. The first craft was similar to the classic "flying saucer" descriptions of a UFO, with the typical circular disc shape. The second craft was following the first, and while somewhat circular, it featured large panels at regular ninety-degree angles, much like the sails or arms of a windmill.

Both of the discs were tilted slightly toward the observer, so he was able to view their top surfaces. The more circular craft had a raised upper portion or deck. This was circular as well and followed the contours of the disc. The windmill-shaped object had a raised upper portion, but it was square instead of circular. Due to the distance, no windows or other details could be made out.

The two objects moved silently and appeared to be one or two kilometres distant from the astonished ballplayer. They were observed in flight for a period of approximately two minutes, and then vanished below the hills, not to reappear.

Were these alien spacecraft, piloted by an extraterrestrial crew? Or some of the Little People out for an evening spin, in the boats from Newfoundland folk tales that sailed without wind and water? Next time you are driving down to catch the ferry in Port aux Basque, keep one eye on the road, and one eye on the horizon. The truth, after all, might be out there somewhere.

JACK THE LANTERN
SHOE COVE BIGHT
NOTRE DAME BAY

AROUND LA SCIE, THE OTHERWORLDLY GLOW of the will-o'-the-wisp is recognized as none other than Jack the Lantern. Not far from La Scie is the community of Shoe Cove. It is about ten kilometres southwest of Cape St. John, the western headland of Notre Dame Bay. The Cove itself is a steep-sided, open bight about two kilometres wide.

Today the Cove is a much different place than it was before Confederation. Before the days of Joey Smallwood and the pains of resettlement, there were many smaller settlements including Stage Cove, The Bight, The Brook, Caplin Cove and Beaver Cove. Since Confederation, most of these sites have been abandoned. One of these abandoned sites, The Bight, was said to be a favourite stomping ground of Jack the Lantern.

Growing up in Shoe Cove Bight, forty or fifty years ago, the young men of the settlement heard the old fellows talk about Jack the Lantern. Skeptics to a man, the youngsters never put much faith in any of the stories. One of the older men who kept the legends alive lived down by the shoreline, and he claimed that he had met Jack the Lantern first-hand.

Years earlier, this gentleman had seen a light coming in from the water. Thinking it was a boat coming in to land on the beach, he went down to meet it. He watched the light come in, but when it came close, its forward movement slowed. In fact, the light did not land on the beach at all. Instead it chose to move parallel to the shore, just the same as if it were a man with a lantern in his hand, walking on the water.

Time and again they heard the tales. But the young men considered the stories told around hot stoves and in the camaraderie of the fishing sheds nothing but old foolishness, and they paid their elders no heed. If they thought of Jack the Lantern at all, they must have figured they were just as likely to meet the Man in the Moon himself, with his own lantern, dog and bush of thorn.

One night around September, a group of three or four of the boys were over in La Scie. The terrain between La Scie and Shoe Cove Bight made overland travel all but impossible, so the boys were used to taking a punt and rowing home.

The boys set off in the punt. When they looked up along the shoreline, they all saw a light upon the water. As they came out into the water a little farther, the light started to come down closer to them. When it got alongside of them it shone dimly in the night, like the low glimmer of a dull flashlight.

The light came close to the bow of the rowboat, and there it stayed, matching the speed of the vessel. One of the fellows, more

Shoe Cove Bight, shown here in the 1940s, was home to a strange type of spirit called the Jacky Lantern. (Courtesy of Kevin Martin)

brave or more foolish than the rest, tried to reach it with the paddle. No matter how hard the lad tried, he could not get handy to the glow. The light remained tantalizingly out of reach, silently hovering only about five or eight feet away, bobbing out of striking distance of the paddle.

When the boys reached the Bight, they turned in toward shore and the more familiar lights of home. At that time there was no wharf, and the locals of the Bight used to tie their craft off on the collar, a place near shore where boats were moored for safety.

The light was persistent in its attention, or perhaps it was curious as to what would take a punt full of young men all the way from La Scie to Shoe Cove Bight so late in the evening. For whatever reason, the light followed the punt to where the boats of the settlement were on the collar. As they turned in toward land, the light apparently thought better of its bold advance and turned out, away from shore.

Where the light had been small and dim all the time it had followed the punt, it now started to change and swell. As it moved off into the distance it got both bigger and brighter. When it reached a spot approximately half a mile offshore, it had grown significantly in size and luminescence.

Looking back, the boys were witnesses to an unbelievable sight. The tiny flame-light glow had metamorphosed into a burning mass of light. As they watched, the light changed into something that looked like a ship all lit up, or a schooner sailing past with its lights lit, and lights all up along the masts and rigging.

They tied up the boat and made their way to their respective homes, minds awhirl with the events of the evening. Much later, the boys spoke of what had happened and of their meeting with Jack the Lantern, and if they were not believed at the time, that perhaps was their reward for their being so disbelieving in the first place.

CANDLEMAS DAY TOKEN
COBBS ARM
NEW WORLD ISLAND

M ARLENE MEADE IS A NEWFOUNDLANDER currently living in Brampton, Ontario. Originally a Burt from the community of Summerford, near Twillingate, Marlene has many memories of growing up in Newfoundland. One of those memories is of a true ghost story that her Dad told her when she was a child. She remembers, "It always gave me goosebumps whenever I heard it."

When Marlene's father was in his late teens he began dating a woman from another small town around Twillingate called Pikes Arm, a woman who would eventually become Marlene's mother. Like many young sweethearts, they took the opportunity of time alone to go courting, as it was then called. They would sometimes go to a community just outside Pikes Arm, park, and talk.

One winter around the year 1963, her father drove from Summerford over to Pikes Arm to pick up his girlfriend. He was driving his own car, a 1950s-model Volkswagen. The twosome parked on a small road across from a bog. It was a very quiet, deserted little road, and there was not another car to be seen.

As the two sat talking, they noticed a light out on the bog coming toward the car. As the light came closer, they thought that perhaps someone was lost. The light came right up close to the car and shone right through the windows.

The young man jumped out of the old Volkswagen and asked, "Do you need help? Are you lost?" When he did this, the light travelled around to the back of the car and suddenly vanished. There was not a soul in sight.

The strange disappearance of the light, coupled with the fact that there was no one to be seen, scared them both. Marlene states,

"My mom is still alive and she recalls that she and my father were both petrified when this happened."

The young man jumped back in the car and beetled off, driving madly back to Pikes Arm. When they reached the girl's house, the scared couple related their tale, and both of them swore it to be true. After they had told the story to the young woman's family, Marlene's grandfather informed them that they were not the first to see the strange light, and he explained the history behind its appearance.

Many years before, there had been a "time" at the lodge in Cobbs Arm. The time was held in celebration of what was known locally as Calmus Day. Calmus Day, February 2, is perhaps better known as Candlemas Day. Folklorist and regular contributor to the *Downhomer* Philip Hiscock says that there are a dozen or so variants of the name for Candlemas Day, including his favourite, Camels' Day!

The name of Candlemas Day is derived from the tradition of blessing the annual supply of church candles on that date. According to the *Dictionary of Newfoundland English*, Candlemas Day is a day for festivities, with singing, dancing, drinking and a meal. There is also the tradition of the Candlemas Cake, which can be an actual cake, or the name for the party held on that special day.

In local folklore, February 2 is a day which will foretell the weather for the months ahead. As the old Newfoundland saying goes, "If Candlemas Day be clear and fine, the rest of winter is left behind; if Candlemas Day be rough and grum, there's more of winter left to come."

The Candlemas Day in question was apparently rough and grum indeed. While the locals of Cobbs Arm were enjoying their Candlemas Cake and all the good fun that came with it, a heavy blizzard came on. All the people present decided to stay in the lodge where it was warm and safe, except one contrary soul who felt like going home.

By this time, the blizzard was so bad that it was impossible to see a hand in front of one's face. But this man's mind was made up in spite of the foul weather, and he would listen to none of the people who tried to dissuade him from his journey. He lit his lantern, stepped out the door, and vanished into the howling whiteness.

The next morning when everyone left the lodge, they found out that the man had not arrived safely home. A search party was pulled together, and the citizens of the community began to hunt for the lost man. Eventually they found his body out on the bog, frozen stiff in the icy grasp of death. The lantern was still clenched between his white fingers. General consensus was that he must have lost his bearings in the storm, and that he froze to death alone in the night.

Many people have seen his light, and it is said that his soul is still wandering the bog. When he learned that the light he had seen was the lantern of the man found dead, Marlene's father was even more terrified than he had been before. Marlene relates, "My dad said that after he left Mom's house that night to go home, if he had gotten a flat tire he would have come home on the rims, because he would have been too scared to get out and change the tire!"

THE FREEMASON'S GHOST
CATHEDRAL STREET
ST. JOHN'S

———

THE THREE-STOREY MASONIC TEMPLE on Cathedral Street in St. John's is arguably the finest lodge of its type in Newfoundland and Labrador. It is an excellent example of Victorian construction, and incorporates classical motifs. It also features many designs particular to the Freemasons, including the large eye in the main triangular pediment which keeps watchful vigil over the street below.

The Cathedral Street Temple was not the first Lodge in St. John's. The Masons had built their first formal Lodge a short distance away on Long's Hill in 1885. Sadly this earlier building was constructed of wood and was one of the early victims of the Great Fire of 1892.

The historic St. John's Masonic Temple was the site of a very public paranormal visitation in 1999. (Courtesy of the City of St. John's Archives)

Prudent men all, the Masons had the foresight to insure the building, and the $28,000 they received in insurance helped to finance the erection of the current Temple. Nervous of another fire, they decided to replace the burnt wooden structure with one of a more durable material. The new Temple was built of Accrington brick, with internal brick supports, a stone foundation, and wooden roof and flooring. The first meeting was held in the Temple on November 1, 1896, but the order did not actually consecrate the building until April 23, 1897.

The main room of the Masonic lodge, to this day, has an elaborate pipe organ, and the interior boasts many other fine details and furnishings. The Temple also boasts a rather unusual ghost story. And unlike many ghost stories, the unexplained events that define it took place in front of a large number of witnesses, including a judge.

On August 7, 1999, possibly for the first time in the Temple's long history, a wedding was carried out inside the sanctity of the smaller of the two lodge rooms on the upper storey of the building. The room was on the north side, closest to Gower Street, with bricked-up windows.

The ceremony was permitted due to rather special circumstances. The groom's grandfather had been a senior member of the Masonic order. He had also been one of the highest-ranking Freemasons of his generation. Sadly, the gentleman had passed away before his grandson could marry. In his honour the ceremony was permitted to be carried out inside the Lodge.

The judge who was presiding over the nuptials entered the room to start the ceremony. He entered with a lit candle and walked across the room toward the spot where the bride and bridegroom were standing. The judge reached a point halfway across the windowless room and the candle went out.

The judge retraced his steps to the back of the room. Once there, he relit the candle and proceeded once more toward the bridal party. Once more, inexplicably, the candle went out when he reached the exact same spot.

At that point the judge walked the remaining distance, lit the candle from the front of the room, and proceeded with the wedding.

After the wedding was over, guests began to talk about the strange business with the candle. It was not long before someone's eyes opened to an intriguing coincidence. What was truly noteworthy about the incident was the location where the candle was twice extinguished. The spot happened to fall directly between two pictures of the groom's grandfather, which hung on opposite walls.

Coincidence? Or perhaps a visit from a loving relative, returning to attend a wedding from beyond the grave? No clear answer exists, and the shade of the ghostly grandfather has not haunted the room since.

THE BURNING STUMP
MILTON, TRINITY BAY

THE TOWN OF MILTON WAS ORIGINALLY known as King's Cove, and was long regarded as a good site for logging. In the 1760s, Benjamin Lester noted in his diaries that families from Trinity used Milton as a site for winter logging operations.

Geoff Adams grew up in the community, and on a number of occasions worked at his uncle's gas station. His uncle was a man in his eighties in the late 1970s, and being something of a storyteller, he often treated Geoff to some of the local folklore. One of the stories was about a stump that burned with a ghostly light.

One night, the uncle had been making his way home from the nearby town of George's Brook. The journey took him up over a hill, and past the United Church and cemetery. It then took him down over the hill, and back into the town near the Pelley Brickyard.

The brickyard was established in 1886 by Charles Pelley, under the name of C. & M. Pelley.

The plant soon became the largest supplier of bricks for the Island's construction industry. Pelley got a major boost from the

Newfoundland Prime Minister William Whiteway, who built his law office out of Pelley brick. By 1898, the brickyard was producing approximately 60,000 bricks per year.

At the crest of the hill overlooking the brickyard, the uncle slowed his footsteps as he became aware of a strange glow coming from the woods. As he got closer he noticed a stump of wood engulfed in ghostly flames. The stump glowed in the darkness of the night, surrounded by a surreal halo of white light.

Adams had never seen anything so eerie in his life. Too scared to investigate further at that hour, he vowed to return the next day to examine the luminescent stump. The next day he returned, only to find a simple rotting stump with no signs of scorching or damage from the inferno of the night before.

Other examples of glowing wood have found their way into folklore and mythology. Aristotle wrote of the phenomena, calling it "cold fire," but more recently it has been termed "fairy fire" or "fox fire." It also makes a brief appearance to lend an air of dread to a scene in Beowulf, the oldest surviving piece of English literature.

It is possible that fox fire has nothing to do with ghosts or the fairy folk, but rather with a genus of fungus known as Armillaria, which may glow at night with a cool, blue-green light. If you open a piece of wood with advanced decay caused by Armillaria, and view it in the dark, you stand a good chance of seeing the luminescence. While the light is not likely to cause blindness, some species are reportedly quite bright.

According to the **forestpathology.org** Web site entry on Armillaria, "it certainly is a wondrous thing to see in the night, bringing a strange mix of delight and spookiness. So it is easy to imagine strange and magical things behind it."

The fungus Armillaria does occur in Newfoundland. Is it possible that some of the local varieties of Armillaria are luminescent? If so, this could explain the mystery of Milton's haunted stump.

CHAPTER 4

Thar She Glows!
Ghost Ships and Sea Dogs

THE SS BLUE JACKET
CONCEPTION BAY

THE GHOSTLY REMAINS of the SS *Blue Jacket*, when seen wreathed in spectral flames, are said by some to be a sign of impending death. One colourful version of the story of the *Blue Jacket* was printed in 1977. The anonymous author wrote:

"The *Bluejacket* was an old British warship that was wrecked near Bell Island about ninety years ago. All hands were lost and for months afterwards the bruised and broken bodies of dead sailors were washed ashore on the rocks at Lance Cove, the last to be found was the body of the Captain still dressed in his brilliant uniform."

While this version of the tale is both heartbreaking and somewhat gruesome, it is a good example of a storyteller not letting the truth stand in the way of a good story. In reality, the *Blue Jacket* was not a British warship, all hands were not lost in the wreck, and instead of going down with the ship, the captain was off even before all the crew and passengers!

The real version of the sinking of the *Blue Jacket* is a gripping tale of survival at sea. The story has been passed down from generation to generation, and there are many people who have kept the tale alive. By far the best and most complete retelling of the sinking of the *Blue Jacket* is found in Volume III of Frank Galgay and Michael McCarthy's *Shipwrecks of Newfoundland and Labrador*, and fans of nautical history are encouraged to read their account.

On Wednesday, September 17, 1862, the day of the sinking of the SS *Blue Jacket*, *The Standard* and Conception Bay *Advertiser* noted that the fare from Portugal Cove to Harbour Grace, Carbonear or Brigus was six shillings for a cabin, or four shillings for general steerage, weather permitting. Passengers like Mrs. Foley of Brigus, who paid out their six shillings in Portugal Cove that day, had little idea of the terror the trip would bring.

The *Blue Jacket*, a small steamer, left Portugal Cove at 12:30 P.M. with a crew of seven and twelve passengers. The wind was high and soon increased to gale force. About three miles from Brigus, the *Blue Jacket* began to list to starboard. The port boiler had gone dry, and the captain ordered the crew and passengers to redistribute the freight to compensate.

When the balance of the ship had been restored, smoke began to pour up from below decks. The overheated boiler had caused nearby woodwork to ignite. The captain gave the order to shut down the engines, but the fire had a head start and soon burst through the decking.

Without power, the *Blue Jacket* was broadside to the wind, and the waves made it difficult to launch the longboat. Several accidents occurred while it was being loaded, but fifteen of the nineteen were placed aboard, too many to be truly safe in high seas. Furthermore, the longboat had a set of paddles, but only one oar and no oarlocks.

When the boat was launched, it was realized that Mrs. Foley and the engineer had been left behind. The captain urged the boat to return for more people, but the people on board refused. He waited for ten minutes, and when no craft came, he and the young cook launched a small dinghy, which filled with water. The captain and the cook bailed her out repeatedly, but she kept filling up. When Mrs. Foley saw the boat leaving, she went to throw herself in the water, but Captain Whittle told her that if she did, he wouldn't be able to save her from drowning.

The fire increased in intensity. The captain was forced to leave Mrs. Foley and the ship's engineer behind on the burning wreck, Mrs. Foley's screams of terror ringing out over the sound of the flames and the howling of the storm. They set off for the longboat, begging it to stay close in case the dinghy was swamped. The longboat still refused to stop, and one passenger was said to have roared out "It's no time now to be looking out for others. It's every man for himself."

Both small boats made it safely to Kelly's Island, where they met up with a fishing skiff under the command of Mr. Henry Gosse. The captain begged him to return for the two left on *the Blue Jacket*, and he agreed, even though he felt it was impossible to save them. Mr. Gosse later recounted his story for the Harbour Grace paper:

"It was a dreadful scene to witness, a helpless female kneeling on the stem with her arms flung open and screaming in a dreadful manner; the steamer was about three hundred yards from the shore with the sea dashing against her, and every part of her, but the stem, on fire."

Against all odds, Mr. Gosse and his crew rescued poor Mrs. Foley. Of the engineer, Mr. Henderson, there was no sign. Mrs. Foley reported he had taken a lifebuoy and thrown himself into the sea. His body was never found.

Over the years it was not the sinking of the *Blue Jacket* that became famous, but rather the life of the ship after its fiery demise. The *Blue Jacket* became one of the most famous ghost ships in Newfoundland folklore. Greta Hussey, the author of *Our Life on Lear's Room, Labrador* and native of Hibbs Cove, Port de Grave, told me that local tradition holds that for years after her sinking, local people could see the *Blue Jacket* out in the bay, going down all ablaze.

Even her father had seen the ghost of the *Blue Jacket*. He had been out on the fishing grounds when the phantom ship appeared. The crew was certain it was the *Blue Jacket* coming. The ghostly vessel was headed straight for them, but before it reached their location, it vanished. There was not a sign to mark the location of her appearance and disappearance.

Mona Petten, who works with the Porter House museum in Port de Grave, offered a little bit of local folklore about the ship. The old people in the area used to say that before a storm they would see the *Blue Jacket* sailing up the bay. The ship could be seen from Port de Grave, and while it was generally believed that it foretold bad weather; other people said it foretold a death.

The enthusiastic 1977 writer suggests that "it seems that the sight of the dead ship with its spirit crew is too much for human flesh and blood to bear, and death comes as a happy release to close forever the eyes that have gazed on the forbidden sight." Melodramatic stuff indeed! The author goes on to postulate that if the *Blue Jacket* is seen moving toward the viewer, death is very near. If the ship is seen moving away from the viewer, the lucky soul then has at least a month left to prepare for his or her inevitable departure from this realm. The idea that it foretold a coming storm somehow pales in comparison.

As Greta Hussey told me, at one point there was nothing strange about seeing the *Blue Jacket* going by. Certainly many have seen it without requiring the "happy release" of death. So if you do catch a glimpse of it next time you are driving along the Baccalieu Trail, I wouldn't worry too much about your allotted time on Earth. But you still might want to get out your rain jacket and umbrella.

THE CHANCE COVE MYSTERY
CHANCE COVE, SOUTHERN SHORE

T ODAY, ONE OF THE MANY ATTRACTIONS for visitors to the Southern Shore is Chance Cove Provincial Park. A hiking trail leads down to the coast where one can see whales, seabirds, and the odd seal along a spectacular coastline. In season, Chance Cove Brook offers good angling for sea-run brown trout. The park also offers visitors a chance to explore the remnants of an abandoned community with a mystifying history.

There are many strange tales told about Chance Cove and many explanations for its mysterious reputation. All the stories, however, seem to share a common point of origin. The event that got the paranormal ball rolling, so to speak, happened way back in 1863 with the tragic wreck of a steamer named the SS *Anglo Saxon*.

The *Anglo Saxon* was a fully-rigged, three-masted steamship built by W. Denny and Brothers of Dumbarton, Scotland, in 1860 for the Allan Line Steamship Company. At the time of the disaster, Baine Johnston and Company was the agent for the Allan Line. The ship was a ten-knot iron vessel used in the emigrant trade from Great Britain to the Canadian West. On April 16, 1863 she left Liverpool, England, with eighty-four crew members and 360 passengers for Londonderry, Ireland, and Quebec City.

On April 27, she attempted to round Cape Race in a dense fog. Around noon, the vessel struck the shore firmly between the twin rocks of Clam Cove, near Chance Cove. Two hours afterwards, the deck caved in. William McMaster, chief engineer of the *Anglo Saxon*, gave his testimony of the accident in the St. John's *Daily News* on April 30. Describing the final moments of the ship, he said

"I then came on deck, and assisted in rigging out a studding sail boom from the ship's rail to an adjacent rock. Over this we succeeded in getting ashore; and then by means of a basket, slung for a chair, we succeeded in getting ashore the women and children. About this time, the ship began to break up. Numbers of the passengers and crew, climbed into the rigging, leaving also a large number on deck, all of whom were drowned. The scene at this time was a dreadful one. We could give them no further assistance, and many of them attempted to save their lives by dropping into the water, but were swept away by the surf. The ship fell over to her port side, and broke completely up, leaving those on board at the mercy of the waves."

The *Anglo Saxon* had on board in all 444 souls. Of these, only ninety-seven were saved. More than a hundred bodies were reported to have been buried on the bank of Clam Cove Brook, Chance Cove.

At the time of the *Anglo Saxon* wreck in 1863 there were no settlers at Chance Cove. Afterwards, the Biar, King and Cunningham families were supposed to have settled near the site of the wreck. The census of 1884 reported fifty-two residents, with seven homes inhabited by seven families on the west side of Chance Cove. At that time the community's main industry was the cod, herring and caplin fisheries, though the livyers also grew potatoes and turnips and were engaged in some boat building.

Chance Cove and the surrounding coastline continued to be well known for the number of shipwrecks which occurred in the vicinity. Local folklore maintains that the inhabitants of Chance Cove may have had something to do with this, as some believe that wreckers were responsible for luring many to their fate.

Whether destroyed at the hands of humans or by act of God, the victims of the many wrecks did not seem to rest easy in their graves. Stories spread of unearthly screams and terrifying apparitions encountered in the town. According to a rather dramatic account, one April evening on the anniversary of the *Anglo Saxon* disaster, ghostly cries and spectral noises erupted in the silence of the night. The men of Chance Cove ran to the beach to see if another boat had suffered the fate of the *Anglo Saxon.* Eerily, the noises stopped, only to resume later with a terrifying intensity.

At some point following this, and for reasons yet unknown, a sudden exodus occurred. Between 1884 and 1891 the settlement was abandoned, and Chance Cove became a ghost town. All inhabitants inexplicably left, leaving homes and farms deserted. A writer named John W. White visited the abandoned settlement in 1897. He found the buildings still standing, and wrote up his impressions in *The Newfoundland Quarterly:*

"For some years previous, up to the summer or fall of 1898, Chance Cove consisted of a number of untenanted dwelling houses, neglected lands, cellars, etc., and the usual appurtenances to the fisherman-farmer abode. No one could give any valid reason why the inhabitants had deserted their houses, except that at certain seasons of the year uncanny noises and loud heart-rending screams used to be frequently heard by the villagers; in fact so real and life-like did they seem to be that the fishermen would sometimes hurry out of bed and away to the beach only to find that nothing was there beyond what might be seen every day."

The abandonment of the settlement was certainly a dramatic one. One author has argued that "following a series of disastrous years in the fishery, practically the entire community in great disgust moved away to Maynard, Massachusetts, leaving their houses, furniture, bridges, stages, boats and gear behind them just as they were."

The idea that something unearthly had driven the people away persisted. As John W. White wrote, "the houses, at least most of them, are in splendid condition, and it can't be poverty that drove them away. Then what did? Is it true that the inhabitants of the other world—if such there be—pay odd visits or pay continuous ones to the place?"

By 1899, the community had vanished completely. A number of northern fishermen, who had been fishing in schooners along the Southern Shore in the summer of 1898, had gone ashore at Chance Cove. They used the houses all season and then set fire to them in the fall, burning the frightening community to the ground.

In the early 1970s, Chance Cove was made a Provincial Park over 2,000 hectares (5,000 acres) in size. Today the former community is identifiable through foundation remains, naturalized vegetation, old cellars, and a graveyard overgrown by spruce forest. Curiously, it has no tombstones and local folklore holds that its population was "buried standing up."

The Chance Cove ghost stories continue to be told. Residents of the Southern Shore have reported the appearance of strangers, cries of people calling for help, and the ringing of a ship's bells, especially on the anniversary of the shipwreck. It is a mystery that continues to amaze, even after almost 140 years since the wreck of the ill-fated *Anglo Saxon.*

THE RETURN OF THE STANLEY PARSONS
HALL'S BAY, NOTRE DAME BAY

THE ILL-FATED STANLEY PARSONS was a freighting schooner from Lushes Bight, near Bay of Islands. Skippered by Sidney Parsons, the schooner made frequent trips back and forth to St. John's.

At some unknown point between December 6 and December 12, 1932, the *Stanley Parsons* vanished without a trace. Yet while the actual *Stanley Parsons* never made it to port, its ghostly remains were said to do so.

The first part of the tale is well documented in Robert Parsons's book *Survive the Savage Seas.* The disappearance of the *Stanley Parsons* is one of many he recounts in the book, and is a sad reminder of countless tragedies played out through the history of Newfoundland and Labrador.

The *Stanley Parsons* was built in Boothbay, Maine, in 1884. Originally named the *Lelia E. Norwood*, she was constructed with a durable oak bottom. In 1923, Skipper Jobie Parsons of Lushes Bight purchased the vessel, fitted it out with new stanchions, rails, deck, deck beams, and christened it with a new name.

On Monday, December 4, 1932, the *Stanley Parsons* left St. John's bound for Notre Dame Bay. The ship was laden with general cargo, including barrels of flour and sugar, vegetables and shop goods. By December 12 the schooner was overdue and the owners were certain it had reached neither Catalina nor Seldom, two of its scheduled stops.

Captain Ernest Burry of Safe Harbour was the last man to see the *Stanley Parsons*. He sighted the vessel at midnight on December 5, off Catalina, about one mile astern of his own vessel, the *Athlete II*. After that, he did not see the *Stanley Parsons* again. Several other ships searched the area, but no wreckage was ever found. None of the men on board were ever seen again.

Those on board were all from Lushes Bight, Long Island, Notre Dame Bay. The crew included the captain, Sidney Parsons, the mate, James Maye, the cook, Uriah Miller, and the deckhands, Cecil Hollett, Thomas Caravan, and his younger brother Wesley Caravan. Apart from the deckhands, all the crew had wives and children waiting for them. The seventh person on board was a passenger named Alwin Parsons, who owned a store in Lushes Bight. He had travelled to St. John's to buy winter provisions for his business, and was on his way back home to his wife and two children.

The verifiable facts of the story end there, supported by contemporary newspaper accounts and research by historians like Robert Parsons. But for our purposes, this is where the story starts to become decidedly more otherworldly.

The loss of the *Stanley Parsons* was certainly a shock to the members of the community and the families of those men who were lost at sea. Imagine what their shock then must have been like when rumours began to circulate that the ghostly remains of the *Stanley Parsons* had been sighted in Hall's Bay!

According to legend and hearsay, a phantom schooner began to haunt Hall's Bay sometime after the unaccountable disappearance of the *Stanley Parsons*. The ghost ship was observed sailing from Long Island all the way to the dock at the community of South Brook.

The legend of the ghost ship goes on to say that the ship seemed to be as solid as any other ship afloat. One eyewitness in South Brook watched the strange ship dock, and then started toward the dock to help the deckhands tie it up. As the man neared the dock to lend his assistance, the ship disappeared in the blink of an eye. If it was indeed the *Stanley Parsons*, it had vanished a second time as mysteriously as it had the first.

THE OLD MAN IN THE MOUNTAIN
CORNER BROOK, HUMBER VALLEY

———

ONE OF CORNER BROOK'S MOST ENDURING and well-known legends is that of the Old Man in the Mountain, a strange face which can be seen in the cliffs outside of the town. The Old Man himself is located just east of the city and is best seen when travelling east to Steady Brook. About two minutes outside of Corner Brook is a rocky cliff known as Breakfast Head. If you slow down and look up, the Old Man in the Mountain can be seen on the rock face overlooking Shellbird Island in the Humber River.

It is often said that the face is hard to locate, but patience and a bit of imagination is all it takes to find it. The Old Man resembles the face of a fisherman or pirate, or Beothuk, depending on who tells the tale. The face leers out over the Humber, looking down on Shellbird Island from his lofty, rocky perch. Legend has it that the Old Man was carved into the mountain to serve as a marker for an undiscovered treasure.

Shellbird Island is situated in the Humber River Valley, the main arterial route between the granite hills surrounding Corner Brook and the only transportation link for east-to-west land traffic in the area.

Captain Cook explored this river valley in 1767, and found Corner Brook to be an excellent base of operations for his work in charting the coastline. Cook was marine surveyor of Newfoundland from 1763 to 1767. Cook's maps were the first to use accurate triangulation. Much of his work was so accurate that many of his charts could still be used today. He went on to explore much of the Pacific and was killed in Hawaii in 1779. If only he had stayed in Newfoundland!

Although Cook was probably familiar with Shellbird Island, there is no indication that the legendary treasure is his. Indeed, the legend states that the treasure was buried by the Spanish or by pirates, and that it was one of them who carved the mysterious face.

The theory that the treasure has Spanish origins may have some basis in reality, as the Spanish were frequent visitors to the west coast of Newfoundland long before Captain Cook started his chart-making work there in the eighteenth century. The Spanish fishery in Newfoundland and Labrador, especially that originating from Basque ports, peaked between 1570 and 1580.

In 1578, Anthony Parkhurst, an English explorer and merchant, reported one hundred Spanish fishermen working in Newfoundland. Tensions between England and Spain, however, contributed to a decline in the industry, with Spanish ships becoming targets of pirates and privateers. As English and French ships came to the Island more often, the Spanish abandoned the Avalon Peninsula in favour of the south and west coasts.

Spain's involvement in the Newfoundland fishery was fated not to last. Harassment of Spanish vessels by pirates and the

English meant that by 1597 Spain relied on the French Basques for supplies of Newfoundland cod.

The busy fish trade, and the even richer fur trade between New France and Europe, proved to be an excellent hunting ground for pirates. And Newfoundland's long-unprotected coastline, with hundreds of hidden bays, made the Island a perfect spot for pirate hideouts.

The west coast, well away from the more densely settled east coast, was ideal hideout territory. Several years before Cook arrived, the west coast was the base of operations for one of piracy's most legendary and bloodthirsty couples, that of Eric and Maria Cobham. In 1740, the pair arrived near St. George's, within easy striking distance of the St. Lawrence River trade routes. The Cobhams were mainly interested in furs, which brought a high price on the black market.

Maria was part of her husband's expedition to Newfoundland and lived here from 1740 to 1760. It is claimed that she was the first European woman to have lived on the west coast of the Island. She was also a ruthless pirate. Maria and her husband made a point of sinking every ship they captured, and killing everyone on board to be certain there would be no witnesses. Ship owners assumed their ships had been lost at sea, with all hands, due to natural disasters.

While the Cobhams used Sandy Point, St. George's Bay, as their base of operations and not Corner Brook, their buccaneering enterprise is proof of an established history of piracy on the west coast. But is the Shellbird Island treasure theirs? Other researchers have argued that the treasure is related to the most famous pirate in Newfoundland history, Peter Easton.

In 1989, authors Frank Galgay and Michael McCarthy published a book entitled *Buried Treasures of Newfoundland and Labrador*, now sadly out of print. In the book, they devoted a short chapter to the Shellbird Island treasure.

Peter Easton, well known on the east coast of the Island for his pirate fort at Harbour Grace, was also active on the west coast. Like the Cobhams, Easton was well aware of the riches to be gained by plundering the merchant ships engaged in the fur trade of New France. Easton intercepted several merchant ships from Quebec City and Montreal, and made quite an impressive haul before being sighted by a French warship.

Easton and his crew realized they were outgunned by the French ship, so they quickly set sail back to Newfoundland. Easton made his way to the mouth of the Humber River to hide from the French. According to legend he decided to bury his treasure, just in case.

The gold was divided into three chests, and Easton entrusted a mate to take the gold and another sailor in a small boat to Shellbird Island to bury it. In one version of the story, the Old Man in the Mountain was already there, and Easton decided to use it as a marker to remember where the gold was buried.

The mate and sailor buried the gold on the island. As the sailor started to fill in the last of the three pits, the mate drew his flintlock pistol and fired! The sailor slumped dead over the chest, and he was quickly buried by the mate in order to provide a ghostly guardian for the gold.

Tragedy struck the mate on the way back to Easton's ship. At a section of the Humber called the Devil's Dancing Pool, the boat was swamped. The mate drowned, taking the exact location of the gold with him. Easton, it was said, later returned to Shellbird Island. He left empty-handed, the gold still buried deep beneath the earth, the spirit of the dead sailor left to protect it.

Over the years, rumours have circulated that portions of the treasure have been found. In the late nineteenth century, it was said that one of the three chests was uncovered, and that the gold doubloons inside were shared in secret. Then, around 1934, word spread that a second chest had been uncovered. Once more, the finders shared their gold in secret, leaving one last chest just waiting to be found. Such is the stuff of legends.

There are many who feel the entire story is just that, a legend. These skeptics argue that the image on the cliff is the result of the natural erosion of the cliff, with the "face" just a random collection of rocks and hollows. Certainly, there are many naturally occurring rock formations all across the Island, and indeed, all over the world, that are said to look like people, animals or other objects. There is even another "Old Man in the Mountain" in Hawaii, and another one in New Hampshire.

But what about the legend of the buried gold? If you discount century-old rumours, no gold has ever been found on Shellbird Island. David Cordingly, a naval historian and world-renowned expert on historical pirates, has argued that the whole idea of buried pirate gold is a nineteenth- century invention. Cordingly writes, "Although buried treasure has been a favourite theme in the pirate stories of fiction, there are very few documented examples of real pirates burying their loot."

The idea of buried treasure was made widely popular by the publication of Robert Louis Stevenson's novel *Treasure Island* in 1883, and it has also been a firm part of Newfoundland folklore for generations. Perhaps it has remained such a fixture in our legends and storytelling traditions because of the slim chance that the gold might be real after all. And as long as the Old Man in the Mountain looks down over Newfoundland's own Treasure Island, there is still a chance that one of us will strike it rich.

THE TIME SLIP
LOLLY COVE, FORTUNE BAY

WE OFTEN THINK OF GHOSTS as being souls trapped in one place after death, or the psychic remnants of emotional energy. If we accept this explanation, it is useful for discussing ghosts of individuals, but it does not help to explain things like ghost ships which had no souls to begin with.

One explanation for this type of haunting is that they may be what have been termed "time slips." A time slip is an event which happened in the past, but which might be seen briefly in our time. The event witnessed may actually be from the past, another time-line somehow slipping into or crossing over our own timeline.

In their book *The Directory of Possibilities*, researchers Colin Wilson and John Grant state that one of the most famous time slip cases was reported in 1901. Two English ladies, Charlotte Moberly and Eleanor Jourdain, were walking through the Trianon Park at Versailles, France on August 10, 1901.

There they encountered a number of people in eighteenth-century costume. Jourdain returned five months later and wit-nessed oddly dressed labourers. Further research convinced them they had experienced the park as it had been at the time of Marie Antoinette.

Not to be outdone, Newfoundland had a strange ghostly encounter which could possibly be explained as a time slip. The event was reported in Lolly Cove, in Belle Bay, Fortune Bay, and actually predated the adventures of Misses Moberly and Jourdain by several years. Lolly Cove was the early name for Lally Cove, Fortune Bay, not to be confused with the Lolly Cove on Random Island in Trinity Bay which was renamed Lady Cove. The name Lolly Cove itself apparently originated from a Newfoundland word for slob ice, or soft ice forming in salt water.

The good people of Lolly Cove were mainly engaged in the business of fishing for cod, salmon, herring and lobster. As the story has survived, they were surprised one day when a strange-looking ship suddenly entered their small but well-sheltered har-bour.

The mysterious ship was crewed by dark, foreign men. They anchored their ship and came ashore. The men would not speak to the locals or answer any questions put to them, speaking amongst themselves in a foreign language which was nothing but gibberish to the citizens of Lolly Cove. Indeed, the foreigners ignored the townspeople completely, acting as if they were not even there.

The newcomers set off at a march, proceeding to a spot well outside of town. The locals stayed their distance but followed close enough to watch. Much to their horror, they observed the men turn upon two of their crew, killing them on the spot. They then proceeded to dig a grave and buried the two men.

When the grave was filled in, the strangers returned to their ship. They weighed anchor, and started to sail away. As they did so, the ship seemed to vanish into the air. Neither the ship nor its eerie crew were ever seen again.

Once the men had vanished, some of the local men hurried back to the gravesite. To add to the mystery of the day's events, the townsfolk could not find the freshly dug grave. Instead, they came across a slight depression in the earth, much grown-over and looking like it had been untouched for centuries.

It was reported long after the initial sighting that no one in the area dared to dig at the spot of the indentation, fearful perhaps of what they might find. By 1966, Lolly Cove was deserted, with most of the people resettling to the community of Belleoram. As far as is known, the unearthly grave remains untouched.

ALPHONSUS KELLY
KELLY'S ISLAND, CONCEPTION BAY

———

STORIES OF GOLD AND GHOSTLY GUARDIANS are a firm fixture in the oral traditions of Newfoundland. Another example has been linked to a pirate by the name of Captain Kelly. Some say he was a lieutenant of the dreaded Peter Easton. Others say he was the leader of a group of slaves on a ship sailing past Newfoundland.

Kelly broke his chains and took over the ship, eventually hiding a huge fortune in gold coins on what is now Kelly's Island, Conception Bay.

After Kelly buried his loot, he killed one of his men and tossed the body into the pit on top of the gold. It is said that his ghost remains to guard the treasure. The spirit that stands guard over Kelly's gold is not nearly as bad as the ghost that watches the treasure on Signal Hill. That ghost is a huge African pirate, with no head. The ghost of Kelly's Island is nothing compared to him.

CASEMAN VERSUS THE PIRATES
HARBOUR GRACE, CONCEPTION BAY

EARLY IN THE 1700S, there was a woman of a successful Harbour Grace family who had a log cabin built for her use some miles from the settlement, where she could read quietly and enjoy some solitude. But peace and quiet didn't come easily, as she often heard heavy footsteps circling her cabin. She examined the area but found nothing, not even a footprint.

She told her fellow villagers of the incidents and was told the history of the site. One of the early colonists, a man by the name of Caseman, built his cabin on that very spot. He cleared some land and started to raise crops to support his family. Then disaster struck.

A group of pirates attacked the settlement of Harbour Grace, bent on murder and destruction. They reached the Caseman farm and decided to take Mrs. Caseman and her two teenage daughters away with them as part of their loot.

Mr. Caseman fought back. He killed one of the pirates but was murdered by the rogue's compatriots. The three women were

Harbour Grace, shown here in the late 1800s, is the site of several pirate legends, including the tale of the pirates who murdered a local man by the name of Caseman. (Courtesy of the Heritage Foundation of Newfoundland and Labrador)

taken away and never seen again. For years afterwards, the heavy footsteps which could be heard circling the cabin were attributed to the pirate that Mr. Caseman had killed in defence of his loved ones.

THE TWO TREASURES
CHAPEL COVE, CONCEPTION BAY
AND BOXEY, FORTUNE BAY

NOT TO BE OUTDONE, CHAPEL COVE, near Harbour Main, boasts both a pirate ghost and a ghostly pirate ship. In 1895, three men set out to find a chest of gold rumoured to be buried in Chapel Cove. No sooner had they hit a rusty metal chest than a ghostly galleon appeared in the harbour, with all sails set. The ship crossed the cove and sailed directly toward the trio. The men were terrified and fled the excavation.

In 1909, a brave chap by the name of Tom Campbell went out to try his luck. He managed to find the chest and attempted to pry it open. This time there was no sight of the ship. Instead, a loud noise emanated from the pit Campbell had dug. Then a spectral form rose up out of the pit, seized the crowbar, and broke it in half.

This was enough for Campbell. Yet another man, a train conductor named Spence, had a go, but he was tormented by ghastly moans and strange figures.

There are numerous other locales across Newfoundland and Labrador that boast treasures guarded by piratical phantoms. The community of Boxey, located on the south coast of Newfoundland almost midway between English Harbour West and Coombs Cove, was one such place. In the nineteenth century, Boxey was well known for an opening or "spy hole" in a local rock formation. The hole was used by local sailors to navigate safely amid treacherous rocks in the bay.

According to local legend, a man named Jacob Penney, and his companion, Simon Bungay, ran aground close to the spy hole. It was said that they had been tricked into running their boat up onto the rocks by spirits.

The two men had been on a treasure hunt to haunted Deadman's Bight, just up the coast from Boxey, when the accident occurred. They were able to pull the boat off the rocks and continue the hunt for the buried treasure. Sadly, the twosome arrived at the location of the treasure, but their misadventure on the rocks cost them valuable time. They arrived on the scene just in time to catch a glimpse of the fabulous treasure, before a rock door slammed shut. The treasure was never recovered.

THE DEVIL AND SAM WESTOVER

ST. SHOTTS, SOUTHERN SHORE

———

T HE DEVIL MUST BE GETTING COMPLACENT in his old age, content to sit in his air-conditioned office somewhere in the nether regions of Hades and let his minions do his work for him. It seems that years ago he got out more, making a special point of arriving unannounced at card parties to beat all players. Today he is hardly seen in person at all.

Luckily for the tourist with a passion for the paranormal, Satan did at one point have a great deal of fun here on the Island. Back then he was happy to hop around leaving his unholy cloven footprints on all manner of stones, boulders, and kitchen floors.

Up until the early years of the twentieth century, the Devil was also said to have left another memento of his earthly activities high on the tops of cliffs near St. Shotts. This was said to be the rotting and rusting remains of ships' timbers, the debris left behind after a notorious pirate named Sam Westover had a run-in with the Devil himself.

According to folklore, Westover was a pirate who used to visit the coast of Newfoundland in the early 1600s. Westover would raid the coast to gather supplies, and then would head out to the Atlantic to terrorize the fishermen on the Grand Banks.

At some point in the early 1600s, Westover was said to have attacked the community of Trepassey, which had been a seasonal fishing station for vessels from the Iberian Peninsula and France for about a hundred years previously. It may have even been the site of a plantation promoted by Sir William Vaughan between 1617 and 1636.

In spite of its history, Trepassey was not as prosperous as the community of Ferryland, farther along the coast. After Westover attacked Trepassey he fixed on Ferryland as his next target. The bloodthirsty crew set out that very day.

The weather, however, had other plans for Westover and his crew, and no sooner were they out of Trepassey Harbour than the wind died, leaving the ship dead in the water. The strong tides kept pulling Westover's ship farther and farther away from land. No matter how hard they tried, the buccaneers could not make it to Ferryland.

After six full days of calm, Westover became violently angry. Then in a fit of rage, shaking his fist at the windless sky, he called out to the Devil himself, with a true piratical oath, saying:

"Damnation seize thee! If God will not send me wind, then may the Devil take this ship and tow it straight to Hell!"

Apparently the offer seemed a good one to the Prince of Lies. The day was calm and clear, without a cloud in the sky and with not a breath of wind in the air. Nonetheless, the ship suddenly spun around and headed straight for the cliffs of Cape St. Shotts. Terrified, Sam Westover ordered his crew to drop the anchor.

The corsairs rushed to do his bidding, playing out the anchor chain. Amazingly, however, an anchor and chain weighing over a thousand pounds floated on the surface of the water and didn't slow down the ship at all.

The ship struck the cliffs of Cape St. Shotts with a sickening blast, and amidst a streak of sparks the wreck was lifted right up the side of the rugged cliff. Its timbers and anchor were left perched high at the top of the cliffs as proof of Westover's blasphemy. The remains of the ship were said to be visible well into the early twentieth century.

CAPTAIN RANDELL'S
GHOST STORY

SELDOM-COME-BY, FOGO ISLAND

THERE ARE MANY NEWFOUNDLAND STORIES that involve the mysteries of the sea, or ghosts, or dealings with the Devil, or tales of pirates. It is very rare to find one that involves all of these elements together! Newfoundland author Robert Parsons, whom I would consider something of an expert on nautical yarns, sent this particular tale my way, and I am much indebted to him for bringing it to my attention.

The story was originally printed in William F. Coaker's newspaper *The Fishermen's Advocate*. It was one of the reminiscences of Captain John Thomas Randell, who had a long career as a naval officer but who is perhaps best remembered for his rum-running career during the 1920s. His ship, the *I'm Alone*, was a frequent visitor to St. Pierre and could carry up to 6,000 cases of liquor at a time. In 1929, the US Coast Guard sank the ship off the coast of Louisiana, provoking a minor diplomatic incident.

Randell's ghost story was reported in *The Fishermen's Advocate* the July following the sinking of the *I'm Alone*. According to Randell, it was a true account of a strange, ghostly event he had witnessed first-hand as a fourteen-year-old boy.

Around 1894, a young Randell had gone off to the Labrador to fish with his father, also named John Randell. The crew worked the coast that summer without incident and headed home in the autumn of the year.

Late one night, the ship was making its way through a little run, a channel inside an island, and then they passed by the harbour at Seldom-Come-By. As Randell the younger stood on the deck with his father, they suddenly heard from the shore a ghostly chorus of shrieks and yells. Then, a huge burst of flame shot up out of the darkness. The flame flared with a brilliant light and vanished, leaving behind only an eerie silence.

"Don't anybody speak," ordered the captain.

The crew obeyed and sailed past the spot in silence. Eventually they dropped anchor, and John Randell explained to his son and his crew what they had seen.

As local legend held it, there had been a boy from Seldom-Come-By who went away to sea and became a pirate. Forty years after he left, he returned to the community. While he was rich, he was also hard and embittered, a very different person from the boy the settlement had known all those years before. He settled into his new life onshore, met a local woman, and took her for his wife.

The old pirate then took sick, and his wife nursed him faithfully. One night around ten o'clock, after she had undressed him and put him to bed, she went to the kitchen. She was gone about three minutes and returned to find him missing. The only exits were through a tiny window which was still latched on the inside, or down the stairs and through the kitchen which she had just left.

The man had vanished naked from his bed. No boats were to be seen in the harbour or on the beach, and no footprints were found in the wet soil around the house. Locally it was believed that the man had made a pact with the Devil, and that the Devil had come to claim what was his. The man was never seen again.

Every ten years, however, on the anniversary of the old buccaneer's mysterious disappearance, a strange event was played out on the beaches of Seldom-Come-By. The screams and fire were said to be repeated once every decade, a chilling reminder of the pirate's wicked life and his ill- fated deal with the Devil.

THE HOLLIES AND THE HURRICANE

NORTHERN BAY SANDS, CONCEPTION BAY

IMAGINE THE FOLLOWING, IF YOU DARE. Hundreds of men lost at sea, wrenched from their loved ones by the uncontrollable wrath of nature at its most savage. Then picture, centuries later, those lost souls still singing out in the night, a ghostly choir three hundred strong.

Sound like a trailer for a Hollywood movie, or a tale too impossible to be real? It is neither. Instead, this is the reality of the "hollies," quite possibly one of the most dramatic hauntings in Newfoundland.

The story of the hollies is associated with one of the most tremendous storms on record to ever hit the Atlantic Coast, the Great Hurricane of 1775. It is known today as the Independence Hurricane. The storm was given this name as it took place at the same time as that other great tumultuous event, the American War of Independence.

The origins of the storm are uncertain, but it is possible to recreate its likely path. It probably began as a tropical storm or cyclone, spawned near the equator and then nurtured in the warmth of the Caribbean. It moved westward and then started to gradually move northward along the eastern seaboard, sucking along with it moisture-rich and unstable air.

The tropical cyclone spiralled up toward the east coast with near-perfect timing. Just ahead of its path was a seductive low-pressure system. The two weather patterns flowed together, the warm moist air from the Caribbean beginning a tempestuous dance with its cool, dry northern partner. The two merged, passions flared, and the storm's intensity grew.

Heavy rains began to fall across North Carolina on the twenty-ninth of August and slowly increased to a fevered pitch. The coast was ravaged from Currituck, North Carolina to Chincoteague, Virginia. Wharves and storehouses on the waterfront were devastated, and bridges were borne away by raging waters. At Williamsburg, Virginia, mill dams broke and cornstalks were blown flat. Winds blew furiously.

At Norfolk, Hampton, and York, many ships were damaged and thrown ashore. Approximately twenty-five vessels were shipwrecked and rendered irrecoverable, and with at least that many sailors left dead. The gunship HMS *Mercury* was driven hard aground and was stranded in two feet of water. When the HMS *Liberty* became hopelessly stranded in a river, a number of local patriots boarded her, captured the crew, seized her cargo, and set the ship ablaze.

Farther north, the stage was set for even greater tragedies. A number of vessels had been sent from Britain to work the Newfoundland fishery, and two thousand of their men were to join Sir William Howe in Boston to serve as soldiers as soon as the fishing business was over. Howe, commander of the British forces in America, had dispatched seventeen vessels to Newfoundland to ferry the soldiers southwards.

None of the sailors, most of them from Britain and Ireland, ever made it to Boston. By September 2, the storm had moved north, and in the first week of that month the hurricane attacked the Atlantic region with full force. Instead of Boston, the sailors found themselves transported to a watery tomb. The hurricane drove other boats far out onto the Grand Banks, and smashed small craft like eggs at Saint-Pierre et Miquelon.

The storm hit eastern Newfoundland around September 9, roaring into Placentia and causing extensive damage. The force of the wind drove flood waters three or four feet high throughout the community. In St. John's, the storm tore the roofs from homes and businesses, reducing chimneys to piles of crumbled bricks, and flattening entire buildings.

Three days later, Conception Bay felt the storm's fury. According to local legends around Northern Bay Sands, the squid had come in late that summer in record numbers, and scores of small boats were out jigging in the bay. Over the horizon to the southeast there spread an orange- hued glow, and as the wind grew in strength, the eldest of the seamen grew terrified.

The ocean grew turbulent, and the sea rose twenty feet above its usual height. The fishing vessels did not stand a chance, and scores of boats were hurled to their doom on Northern Bay Sands.

The hurricane continued as far north as Fogo and LaScie, where several more vessels were lost. At that point, the storm's passions cooled. It dissipated, and faded into meteorological history.

Meanwhile, the loss of life was staggering. In total, it was estimated that the Independence Hurricane killed over 4,000 individuals, most of them British, Irish and Newfoundland sailors and fishermen. It was not surprising that some saw the storm as an omen sent from above.

Nathan Hale, an American soldier stationed in Massachusetts, learned of the terrible toll of the storm, and wrote a detailed letter to his wife on December 6, 1775. Regarding a British Lieutenant who had been recruiting soldiers to fight against his fellow American revolutionaries, Hale wrote:

"There is an account arrived here from Halifax that there was a Lieut of the Regulars recruiting there & had recruited one hundred & twenty when the news came to that place & that he said that the people, the wind, the seas, & that God was against them & that he would seal or fling up his Commission for he would not be concerned in so dammed a cause."

Nowhere was the aftermath of the Independence Hurricane more dramatic or eerie than at Northern Bay Sands, where the scene after the storm was one of absolute desolation.

Miraculously, one young cabin boy survived the destruction. The lad had been lashed to the helm of a boat. The strength of the gales whipped up waves so high that the boat was tossed up onto the beach and was wedged between two trees. Thomas English, an Irish planter who lived near the beach, found the lucky lad. English later adopted the boy, and to this day there are still families named English who live in the area. Perhaps some of them are descendants of this survivor.

Others were not as fortunate as the cabin boy. Oral tradition maintains that three hundred men from Conception Bay perished during the storm. When the winds and rains abated, the beach was found to be littered, full of dead bodies. The identities and home ports of these men remain a mystery.

The local settlers buried the waterlogged corpses of the ill-fated men in a mass grave on a bluff overlooking the beach. Their final resting spot was marked with flat stones. Families grieved and time passed. People assumed that, in spite of the tragic loss, life would continue as it had before the disaster.

Time and fate, however, had different ideas. For many years afterwards, the bones of drowned men continued to wash ashore at Northern Bay Sands as a gruesome reminder of the Independence Hurricane. As if the bleached skeletal remains of sailors were not horrifying enough a reminder, it soon became obvious that even more terrifying forces were at work.

Many local inhabitants started to claim that they could hear the cries of the drowning men. The moans and shouts of these tortured souls became known as "the hollies." There were those who believed that the mournful cries made by dead fishermen were often multiplied by the same souls wailing old sea shanties. Those left behind amongst the living learned to interpret the ghoulish noises. If the hollies were heard crying out, it was taken to mean that a big breeze of wind was coming.

The word "holly" has even made its way into the *Dictionary of Newfoundland English*, denoting the cries of dead fishermen heard on stormy nights. In their book *This Marvellous Terrible Place*, Yva Momatiuk and John Eastcott quote one person relating, "I remember my grandfather walking into a house and saying, 'You can pull your boats in; I just heard the old hollies.' And the men went down and pulled up the boats."

Today, it is said the beach where the sailors washed ashore in 1775 continues to be a troubled locale, full of eerie portent. The hollies still cry out in the night to warn of coming storms, and as long as they do, it will be impossible to forget the dire legacy of the Independence Hurricane.

GHOST SUBMARINES?
TRINITY, TRINITY BAY

EVERY COMMUNITY IN NEWFOUNDLAND and Labrador has its own tradition of strange tales, and Trinity, Trinity Bay, is no exception. A number of Trinity's spirits were recorded for posterity in 1925 by William White (1860-1949). A native of Trinity, William White devoted much time in his later years to the collection and recording of local and church history. He also compiled a history of Trinity.

William White documented a number of different ghosts for the community. Some of them would feel quite at home in almost any community, such as the ubiquitous headless man. Others are more unique. One ghost stands out for its strange proportions, for it was said to boast a head as large as a barrel and eyes like saucers.

Another intriguing story falls into the great Newfoundland tradition of ghost lights. Starting around the year 1916, a very brilliant light was seen just a few miles off Trinity Narrows. The light had not been seen before, but was soon a regular occurrence. When it was first seen, the strange light was initially believed to be the lights of an approaching ship. This was soon proved to be not the case at all.

It was written that when the Fort Point lightkeeper first observed the glow, he was convinced it was the SS *Prospero*. One of the ships in the Bowring Brothers' steamship fleet, she was a well-known ship in her day, and the *Prospero*'s best-known master was the mariner and politician Abram Kean.

The lightkeeper, convinced the ship was making an unscheduled stop at Trinity, rowed all the way across the harbour "in great haste" to the public wharf. He reached the wharf to wait for the arrival of the SS *Prospero*, but discovered no sign of an approaching ship.

The community of Trinity, Trinity Bay, was plagued by strange lights during the early twentieth century. (Courtesy of the Heritage Foundation of Newfoundland and Labrador)

The ghostly light became very much talked about. Unlike other phantasms, this one was viewed by hundreds of witnesses. It also displayed astonishing regularity. The light was seen frequently and usually from 9:00 P.M. to 11:00 P.M.

When the light showed no sign of vanishing, the population of the town became very excited.

They feared it to be a German submarine attempting to cut the Atlantic cable or preparing to attack the town. Perhaps sounding strange today, at the time it was a very real fear.

In 1916, the year the light was reported, Great Britain was in the midst of the first Great War. It is estimated that in October 1916, German U-boats sank 337,000 tons of shipping, followed by 961,000 tons of shipping sunk between November 1916 and January 1917. Here in Newfoundland, officials within the Catholic Church held discussions to settle what buildings owned by the Church would be turned into hostels in the case of German submarine raids.

It was not surprising, therefore, that the citizens of Trinity reported the strange lights appearing at the mouth of their harbour to the authorities in St. John's. The authorities looked into the matter, and reported the news to the cable company at Heart's Content. They informed everyone that no one was tampering with the cable.

Still the light appeared, and the ending of the war with Germany brought no end. In the early 1920s, a fisherman on the fishing grounds off Trinity after dark had a close encounter with the light. He saw the light a few hundred yards distant, but as he drew nearer, it vanished.

At the time, some skeptics argued that the happening was caused by the light of a train near Grate's Cove. The more superstitious saw it as the token of a vessel which was lost with all hands. The truth was never discovered.

CHAPTER 5

Ghoul Goulash!
A Paranormal Miscellany

THE GHOSTS OF CORNER BROOK

CORNER BROOK, HUMBER VALLEY

G HOSTS, ALMOST BY DEFINITION, are elusive creatures. They flit in and out of our field of vision and the stories we tell. They are ephemeral beings, and hard to pin down. They keep to the shadows and tend to shun the company of us mere mortals. The ghosts of Corner Brook are no exception.

When I went looking for a Corner Brook ghost story, one of the very first responses I got was that Monaghan Hall is haunted. Monaghan Hall serves primarily as a student residence for the Western Regional School of Nursing and other educational facilities in Corner Brook. In addition to the residence facility, the building houses the nursing school and general administration offices.

Truth be told, I was a little skeptical of this story, almost from the start. Every college residence, university dorm, and frat house in North America must have its own ghost story. These types of urban legends have more to do with late-night attempts to freak out fellow students than they do with documented visitations from the netherworld!

I thought I would try to find a reputable source, and managed to track down a woman at Monaghan Hall who had worked there for over twenty years. She seemed pretty certain that Monaghan Hall is not haunted, and in her twenty years of employment in the building, the only mysterious thing she could report about the place is that pens and pencils kept disappearing from her desk!

She did inform me, however, that there was a rumour a few years ago about the John I. O'Connell Centre. This was the former hospital, and is now a long-term care facility. These tales, unfortunately, had also proved to be unfounded. Today, the O'Connell Centre ghost stories have all died out, so to speak.

Two potential hauntings, vanishing like mist before my eyes. The phantoms of Corner Brook were proving to be elusive indeed!

But better things were in store. Another ghostly anecdote was passed along to me from a former resident of Corner Brook who now resides in Yellowknife, NT. When he was in Newfoundland, this particular gentleman lived on Hillside Road in Corner Brook. Close to where he lived, there was an old path that ran up to Humber Road. Almost at the top of that path, at the end closest to Humber Road, there was an abandoned two-storey house.

The man who told me the story swore that when he and his friends used to walk by this place at night, they could hear odd noises coming from the abandoned house. The strange noises would put the fear of the Lord into them, and away they would run until they reached the safety of their homes. The man was only in the building once, and he only dared to go just as far as the first floor. From what he could remember, most of the furniture was still there, including a big old-fashioned piano in the parlour. Perhaps this had been the source of the noise, with some long-departed pianist tickling the ivories with decaying, spectral fingers.

The history of the house and the identity of its owners are long forgotten, and the building itself burned to the ground sometime around 1968. When the fire died down and all was said and done, only the concrete footprint of the basement was left. But that silent foundation, it was said, still possessed enough strange energy to send shivers down the backs of those walking by.

A very similar haunting is reported having happened over fifteen years ago on Valley Road. A house on the street had been vacant for many years, and it was understandably a source of fascination for local children. Accounts of strange noises emanating from the empty house filtered down the street. Apparently, no one was brave enough to venture into the desolate house and prove once and for all if it was haunted or not!

PORT DE GRAVE'S PHANTOMS
PORT DE GRAVE, CONCEPTION BAY

THERE ARE A NUMBER OF NEWFOUNDLAND place names that have always appealed to the ghoulish side of me. Deadman's Pond and its next-door neighbour Gibbet Hill in St. John's, the wonderfully named Isle aux Morts, and Cormack's Mount Misery, all of these seem perfectly in place when viewed from a certain Gothic perspective. It was with great dismay that I discovered one of my favourite macabre monikers to have in fact a quite mundane origin.

Perhaps it says something about my imagination that I always believed the community of Port de Grave to have something to do with graves. My dark fantasies were cruelly shattered by the *MacMillan Book of Canadian Place Names*, which states that the name Port de Grave is traceable to the French "grève" or "grave" for pebbly or sandy beach. Disappointing, indeed.

My disappointment, however, was somewhat alleviated by the revelation that Port de Grave is reportedly haunted not just by one ghost, but by two at the very least. I remain convinced that the community harbours other ghostly goodies of which I am not yet aware.

The community of Port de Grave is one of the oldest in Conception Bay. Local tradition holds that the Dawe family was a fixture in the area as early as 1595. It is even said that the Dawes ushered a newly arrived John Guy farther along the coast to Cupids in 1610, in order to keep Guy's colonists from interfering with their fishing premises.

Be this historical truth or popular folklore, it remains a good story, and the centuries that have passed have certainly allowed Port de Grave to accumulate many other good (and ghostly) tales. One of these local tales involves that favourite character of fireside yarns worldwide, the headless man.

Headless ghosts were at one point a dime a dozen in Newfoundland. Sandy Point, Bay St. George had one, and the abandoned community of Hebron in Labrador was occupied by a man without a face. Not to be outdone by any outport, St. John's boasted two decapitated phantoms, one off Queen's Road and one on Signal Hill.

The headless person of Port de Grave used to come down a certain lane, after night had fallen, and the lane was left bathed in moonlight. He haunted a specific spot along the lane, close to a well. The well itself was located right in the centre of the path.

Years ago, local children were warned by their grandfathers never to venture up to the well after dark. Whether this was for fear they would meet the fearsome creature, or for fear they would fall into the well in the darkness, is uncertain. Also unknown is how the careless man managed to misplace his noggin in the first place.

Another ghost story is told of an old cooper or barrel maker. These men were among some of the earliest craftsmen to arrive in Newfoundland, as barrels were a key part of the Island's traditional fishery. Coopers would work to make tight barrels for wet goods, slack barrels for dry goods or salt fish, as well as the various tubs, pails, churns, dippers and bailing buckets the settlers and fisherfolk needed.

Port de Grave boasts both a headless phantom, and the spirit of a deceased cooper. (Courtesy of the Heritage Foundation of Newfoundland and Labrador)

One of these craftsmen did not let death interfere with his trade, and long after his earthly passing, he could still be heard hard at work down in the cove. People claimed that the man toiled away eternally, and that the sound of him knocking the hoops onto the barrels could be heard from time to time, ringing mysteriously through the night air.

NEWFOUNDLAND'S MOST HAUNTED STREET
VICTORIA STREET, ST. JOHN'S

WHILE ONE OF THE SHORTER STREETS in downtown St. John's, at a mere three blocks long, Victoria Street has more than its fair share of ghosts and phantoms. This may have something to do with its age, as Victoria Street is one of St. John's oldest. The street was once known as Meeting House Lane, and took its name from the old Congregational Church Meeting House, which stood on the site where the historic Longshoreman's Protective Union (LSPU) Hall is located today, at 3 Victoria Street. The land for the Congregational Church was purchased in 1785 and the Meeting House was completed in 1789.

The LSPU Hall not only sits on the site of the old Meeting House, but its current foundation contains stone from the foundation of the old building. Rebuilt after the Great Fire of 1892, the Hall burned again in the 1920s, and was rebuilt a second time. Since the late 1970s, the Hall has been a focal point for theatrical and musical activity in the downtown area, and in October of 1999, the Resource Centre for the Arts celebrated its twentieth year in the building.

Many people in the theatre community of St. John's have gossiped about the existence of a "presence" within the Hall, a ghostly resident whose possible existence has been discussed for many years. The LSPU Hall's most recent haunting is rumoured to include the spirit of a St. John's man who was active in the arts community.

A couple of years ago, a young St. John's man drowned tragically one night in a pond outside the city. While young in years, the man was a tireless supporter of the arts and local music, organizing community events and concerts. The suddenness of his death left a tangible hole in the downtown arts community. It is possible, however, that his energy and dedication to the scene have not completely dissipated.

Shortly after his death, a female visitor to St. John's attended a live theatrical performance at the Hall. As she sat in the darkness, the woman became aware of a young man seated alongside her. It became obvious from his body language and facial expressions that he was enjoying the production immensely.

As the production drew to its close, and the house lights were raised, she turned toward him to remark on the play, and was startled to find a suddenly empty seat meeting her gaze. Later she recounted the story to someone familiar with the Hall, and as she described the young man's appearance, his long hair and his black leather jacket, it became obvious that she was describing the man who had drowned months earlier.

His shade has been reported not only sitting in the darkened theatre seats, but also standing in the wings of the theatre, half obscured by shadows and curtains, even while performances have been in progress. The next time you take in a performance at the Hall, you might want to take a long second look at the person sitting next to you, for it may be something more, or a lot less, than what you first may wish to believe. The ghost was sighted as recently as September of 2001.

While perhaps startling to inhabitants (or the lucky theatre-goer), most of Victoria Street's ghosts are relatively harmless. A good example of this is the ghost of 23 Victoria Street. An older St. John's man told me in the fall of 1998 that he, as a very young man, had lived at number twenty-three, and while he lived there, so many years ago, he had been surprised by the ghost of an elderly woman. This phantom woman had appeared before him, standing on the landing halfway up the stairs of the house. The house is today divided into different apartments, and whether or not there have been more recent sightings is a question that remains to be answered.

The ghost of the old woman of number twenty-three pales before some of the street's other restless dead. The most well-known and most horrific of Victoria Street's many ghosts are the two made famous by Newfoundland author Jack Fitzgerald. This direful duo are said to haunt a house near the corner of Victoria Street and Bond Street. In the winter of 1907-1908, a Newfoundland couple living in the United States returned to St.

John's, and rented a house on the corner of Victoria and Bond. Upon their first night in the house, the wife was awakened from her sleep by a horrific series of blood-curdling screeches.

Terrified, the woman sat bolt upright and saw the ghostly figure of a woman at the foot of her bed, a woman who had been known to her, but who had died several years before in the very same room.

The Longshoremen's Protective Union Hall on Victoria Street, St. John's, is home to a very theatrical ghost. (Courtesy of the Heritage Foundation of Newfoundland and Labrador)

What was even more terrifying was the fact that the demonic screaming was not coming from the figure of that woman, but from the apparition of another woman she also knew to be dead, who was being dragged by her hair through the bedroom by the first ghost. The wife passed out cold, and could not be revived till daybreak. The couple took their personal belongings, and never set foot in the house again.

According to the St. John's *Evening Telegram* at the time, the landlord refused to refund any of the three months' rent paid in advance. Sadly, the reporter neglected to mention which of the houses on the corner of Victoria and Bond the story concerned.

While this author cannot say for certain which house was the one with Mr. Fitzgerald's hair- pulling and screaming ghosts, there have been more recent (although somewhat less dramatic) visitations in the house on the southeast corner of the intersection of Victoria and Bond.

This house, a three-storey Second Empire house of the style so common after the Great Fire, has had several recent ghostly events associated with it. Only a short number of years ago, the house was being rented out to a group of friends, who shared the space and split the rent between them.

One day, while one of the tenants was at home, he heard someone enter the house and run all the way up the stairs to the top floor, banging a door shut once the top storey was reached. The tenant paid no heed to the noise, taking it to be, as one in his situation well might, nothing more than one of his housemates returning home.

Some time passed, and the man's other housemate came into the house, looking for the third tenant. The man told the newcomer that the housemate in question had come home earlier, and had gone upstairs. However, in true ghost-story fashion, when the searcher went up to find the man in question, the top floor was found to be vacant. Eventually, when the third man did return to the house, he claimed not to have been in the house for the entire day. The footsteps and banging door went unexplained.

The top floor of this house seems to be a focal point for paranormal activity. One night, one of the men was lying in bed when he heard a pounding at the door to his bedroom. He answered the knocking, and found no one there. He returned to bed. No sooner had he done so than the knocking resumed. Once more, by the time he reached the door, the landing was empty.

The man returned to his room, convinced that one of his friends was playing a practical joke. This time when the knocking returned, he ignored it, refusing to fall for the prank. This time, however, the knocking did not stop at the door. The man listened as the knocking started to move from the door to the wall beside it, and then move along the corridor. The knocking continued along the wall to the corner, where the passageway ended at the exterior wall of the house. Then, terrifyingly, the ghostly rapping turned the corner and continued along the outside of the house, from some point in mid-air, three storeys off the ground, and well out of reach of human hands.

THE WATER-WALKING GHOSTS
CHALEUR BAY, SOUTH COAST

IN OCTOBER OF 2001, I WAS TOLD a strange story by a woman from the community of Francois. This woman claimed never to have had a supernatural experience of her own. In spite of never having seen a ghost herself, she was familiar with several true paranormal tales from her area. One of these tales concerns a mysterious couple fated to walk the shore eternally, hand in ghostly hand.

The community of Francois, pronounced and sometimes spelled as "Fransway," is to be found on the south coast of Newfoundland on a strip of land at the head of a steep-walled, rocky fjord. Overlooking the town is an imposing cliff-like hill named "The Friar," which is over two hundred metres (680 feet) in height. In 1839, the Reverend William Marshall, upon viewing the dwellings built at the base of The Friar, declared Francois to be "a curious place."

A man by the name of James Marsden was the first settler in the community, according to the oral tradition of Francois. Marsden was an English immigrant who had first settled in English Harbour, Fortune Bay, and who moved to Francois around 1850. Marsden was joined by other settlers with names like MacDonald, Kelly, and

Inkman. The Durnford family from West Devonshire settled at Francois around 1860, moved away, and then decided they missed the place so much that they moved back around 1880.

Until the early twentieth century, the economy of Francois was based on the summer fishery, with the catch originally sold to the Newman and Company plantation at Gaultois. From November into the spring, many Francois residents wintered at the bottom of Chaleur Bay, east of Francois.

In Chaleur Bay, there was suitable shelter for dories and punts, and the Marsdens, Durnfords and other families made the place their winter home. They kept busy by hunting, fishing and cutting wood. A whale factory was also in operation in the bay from 1893 to 1911.

By the early 1900s, the winter settlements in Chaleur Bay were largely abandoned, leaving only hints of a once bustling place. Not all signs of life have vanished, however. Even today, Chaleur Bay draws people from Francois, and many people from Francois have cabins in the area. More interestingly for us, it is also a spot known for many ghost stories.

One location in the bay where people have built cottages is a place called Cooper's Cove. It seems to be one of the haunted locations in the bay, and several tales circulate about strange late- night visitations.

In July of 1999, the woman who related the story to me was camping with friends at Cooper's Cove. The woman and a friend were staying in a cabin belonging to the friend's uncle, located at one end of the beach. Earlier that day, they had made plans to meet up with two other friends who were bunked down in a cabin at the far end of the beach. By this time it was getting late, and the women were waiting for their guests to arrive.

Outside, the shadows deepened and evening gave way to the stillness of night. Midnight arrived and passed without the arrival of the friends. Suddenly, the two men burst through the door of the cabin, shutting it behind them. The two men were obviously frightened. The women immediately asked them what had transpired out in the darkness of Cooper's Cove beach. The men had been walking along the beach, making their way from one side of the cove to the other. They were walking up above high-tide level, at the point where the sand met the grass. As they walked, they could see two people walking on the beach. They could see that the two figures were holding hands. The couple were about fifteen feet ahead of them, and much closer to the water than the men.

The first thought of the men was that the two figures were, in fact, the two women they had arranged to meet. However, as the two men walked toward them, the couple paid them no attention. As the men drew closer, the two people walked on, maintaining their distance ahead. When the men stopped, the mysterious couple stopped as well.

Still thinking it might be the two women trying to play some prank on them, the two men ducked down into the grasses to see what the people would do. The two people, still holding hands, stood still. Then when the two men stood up again, the two people disappeared before their eyes.

The men hurried toward the spot where the twosome had vanished. When they reached the area where the two people had been standing, they discovered something that caused the hair on the backs of their necks to rise.

Just ahead of where the men had ducked into the grass, they found that the beach jutted inwards into the cove. This meant that the strange couple had not been walking on the beach at all. Instead, they had been walking, hand in hand, on the surface of the water.

The men realized that they had just been witnesses to some-thing far beyond the realm of the ordinary. Terrified, they ran the remainder of the distance along the beach to the safety of the women's cabin.

Before you dismiss ghosts that walk on water as mere fiction, you should know that the Cooper's Cove ghosts are not the only phantoms which have been seen walking on water. Instead, it seems to be a theme reported the world over. Consider the famous case of

"La Llorona," the weeping woman of New Mexico. This water-walking ghost has been witnessed, with arms outstretched, walking on the surface of a New Mexico river, calling for her lost sons, and trying to lure the living into the water.

Do the ghosts of Cooper's Cove have the same dreadful purpose, trying to lure the unwary into the briny deep? Certainly there is a strong tradition of trickster spirits in Newfoundland, like the Jacky Lantern and the Will o' the Wisp, who are always looking for souls to lead into bog holes or over cliffs.

Perhaps instead, the Cooper's Cove ghosts are the non-corporeal remains of lovers from the heyday of Chaleur Bay, and have no evil in mind at all. It is very possible that the line of the beach has shifted and moved with the passage of time. Such a movement might well have no meaning for star-crossed lovers who walked that beach in life, and who are doomed to walk it for eternity, but that is just a theory. The mystery of the Chaleur Bay ghosts may never be solved.

THE HORSE WHO SAW A GHOST
BLACK DUCK BROOK
PORT AU PORT PENINSULA

———

WITH A HISTORY OF EUROPEAN settlement that stretches back to the Basques in the 1500s, the Port au Port Peninsula has heard many a strange tale over the centuries. It has also produced a number of tale-tellers, one of the best known being Emile Benoit.

Emile Joseph Benoit was born in 1913 at L'Anse-a-Canards (Black Duck Brook) on the Port au Port Peninsula, son of Medee and Adeline Benoit. He began playing the fiddle when he was nine, teaching himself to play on a homemade violin. By the time he was seventeen, he was a well- known local entertainer, and he went on to achieve national and international recognition. He was also a respected storyteller, both of personal reminiscences and the older traditional tales.

When he was a young man, Emile had a run-in with a ghost which was visible to horses alone. One weeknight in March, he hitched up his one-horse sleigh and went to visit his brother Ben. Ben lived at Three Rock Cove, a fishing community on the northwest shore of the Port au Port Peninsula. Three Rock Cove was originally named Trois Cailloux, or "Three Boulders," by migratory French fishermen who used it as an outpost.

Emile stayed there for a spell and had supper. After he had dined with his brother, he decided that he would go visit his sister, Yvonne, who lived about a mile away. He told his brother that he would be back at nine o'clock and set out.

The wind was blowing from the northeast as Emile made his way down the pathway. When he got close to his destination, he had to open a gate and go across a field. About two hundred yards farther along was the sister's house, at the top of a rounded hill. He tied up the horse behind the house and gave it a feed of hay.

When he went into his sister's house he found her chatting with some young women around his own age. Engaged in the pleasant company of the young women, he didn't notice the passing of time until he realized that it was already nigh on nine o'clock.

It was a clear, moonlit night as he started back toward his brother Ben's house. By the time he hitched up the horse and turned the sleigh around, the wind had all but died away. He cut a plug of tobacco and started to make himself a cigarette as the horse plodded along. Then the horse stopped.

It was a good horse, and one of which he was proud. Tall and well built, its mother was a racer, and the horse had some of her character. When he bought it, he had paid out two hundred and fifty dollars for the horse, a sizeable sum in those days.

Busily engaged in the work of hunting for a match for the cigarette, he simply told the horse to keep moving. Sure enough, the horse started to move, but not in the direction Emile had intended, for the horse began to back up along the path, retracing its steps.

He told the horse to go on again, but the horse continued to back up.

Puzzled, Emile started to look around to see what was frightening the horse but could not see a thing. He looked along the line of the fence and could see nothing in either direction. It came to his mind that if he looked between the horse's ears he would see exactly what the horse was staring at. Therefore, he got up on the board at the front of the sleigh and looked up over the ears of the horse, but could still see nothing.

With an oath, he reclaimed his seat, took a good hold on the reins, and delivered a blow to the horse with the whip. The horse reared up, turning the sleigh around like a top, and was off like a flash of lightning, back toward the house they had just left.

Completely startled by the horse's actions, he lost the reins. By the time he got them back in his hands, the horse was back at the gate they had passed through shortly before. Emile got out of the sleigh, took the horse by the halter, and started to lead him by hand.

At this, the horse pounded its hooves into the ground, stamping and whinnying—making it clear it would not set foot on the path. When it became obvious that the horse had no intention of returning home that night, Emile gave in and led the beast back to his sister's house.

Somewhat surprised to see him back so soon, his sister asked him what had happened. He related the story, telling her that the horse would not go back along the path. Emile then asked his brother-in-law Fintan if he would go back with him. Fintan refused to go and then told him a strange tale.

Apparently the mailman had also tried to move his horse along the same path the same night with the mail. At the same point, his horse had refused to move and had turned around the same way. The mailman was stuck, and had to find shelter for the night with one of the local families.

When Emile tracked down the mailman and asked him if he would go out and try again, the mailman refused. So, two cows were taken out of the barn and turned out into the field for the night, and space was made for Emile's horse.

Eager to get home, Emile left around four or five in the morning the next day. The weather was the same as it had been the night before, with not a breath of wind and with a layer of frost on the ground. The horse once more plodded along, and Emile watched his ears, to see if the horse would act up when it reached the same spot.

When they reached the spot the two horses had refused to pass, the ears did not give so much as a twitch. The horse passed by as if nothing had happened, and maintained its usual pace all the way home. The frost on the path showed that nothing had gone before them.

Years later, in the style of a natural storyteller, Emile related the strange occurrence to the folklorist Gerald Thomas. In turn, Thomas included the tale in his book *The Two Traditions*, which deals with the French-language traditions of the Port au Port Peninsula.

Emile never uncovered the reason for the horses' fright. He was certain, however, that whatever the two horses had seen, it must not have been a pretty sight, or anything pleasant, to have frightened them that much. In Emile's own words, "It wasn't God for sure he seen. No..."

According to Ferryland native Ray Curran, horses on the other side of the province had similar experiences. Mr. Curran related that along the Southern Shore there are a number of large rocks alongside roadways said to be possessed by the devil. There was one in Renews and another in Tors Cove. Horses would run away once they approached these sites, and many people were injured as a result of these boltings.

PHANTOM FIRES
WILLICOTT'S LANE, ST. JOHN'S

R UNNING OFF BOND STREET IN DOWNTOWN St. John's is Willicott's Lane, one of the oldest lanes in St. John's. If you had stood on this lane in the early 1800s, you would have been smack in the middle of an area known as Tanrahan's (or Tarahan's) Town. A maze of tightly packed, poorly constructed houses, garbage-filled ditches and open sewers, the area produced a particularly dreadful stench, often offending the delicate nostrils of those attending Sunday Service in all their finery at the Cathedral.

Named after a local slum landlord, the neighbourhood saw some 1,500 souls crammed into about two hundred houses, all of which burned to the ground in the Tanrahan's Town fire of 1855. The neighbourhood was rebuilt from the ashes, only to be destroyed completely a mere thirty-seven years later in the Great St. John's Fire of 1892.

With its history of destructive fires, it is fitting that one of the more unique hauntings in Newfoundland occurs within the limits of what was once Tanrahan's Town. This haunting involves a house which backs onto Willicott's Lane. The building was constructed shortly after the Great Fire of 1892. For most of the middle part of this century, the house was occupied by an old woman who lived alone in the house, and who eventually died within its walls.

The house stood empty for a while before it passed on to new owners who began to notice a very strange phenomenon. A second-floor room on the back of the house contains not the ghost of a person or animal, but rather a ghostly fire. Different people have reported seeing a fire burning in the fireplace, but upon closer examination, the fire has disappeared, and a hand placed within the grate has felt no heat, the stones cold to the touch.

In the 1980s, as a tenant lay in his bed in a different room on the same floor, his door swung open. Looking from his bed out into the hall, the man saw the flickering of firelight reflected on the walls. Knowing himself to be alone in the house, he left his bed to investigate, and found nothing. He closed the door, and returned to bed.

Once in bed, the door swung open again, revealing the same strange light. He got up to check and again found nothing, the light disappearing as he left his room. A third time he returned to bed, and again, just as he was drifting off to sleep, the door swung wide, the firelight flickering on the opposite wall.

While this type of haunting is rare, it is not unique. A similar spirit fire was reported in a small seaside community on the south coast of Ireland by John D. Seymour in 1911. According to reports, a large family house in the community was known to be haunted by a variety of spirits. Two sisters occupied one of the upstairs rooms, where they shared a bed. The two girls on numerous occasions awoke to find the floorboards of the room engulfed in flames, flames which produced neither smell nor heat.

The first time this happened, the girls ran from the room, convinced, as one very well might be, that the room underneath was ablaze. This fire would be witnessed two or three nights in a row, and then would disappear for some time before suddenly blazing forth once more. While it was witnessed on occasion in other parts of the house, it occurred chiefly in the room where the two girls slept.

THESE BOOTS ARE MADE FOR HAUNTING
ST. VINCENT'S, AVALON PENINSULA

———

THE COMMUNITY OF ST. VINCENT'S at the southern end of the Avalon Peninsula has a very long history. It first appeared on Portuguese maps in 1519 and was known as Porta da Cruz. By 1693, it was known by sailors as Holyrode, a name which stuck for more than two hundred years. Up until 1910, when it was christened St.Vincent's, it was called either Holyrood Pond or Holyrood South, to keep it distinct from the Holyrood in Conception Bay.

In 1845, there were eighty-three people living at St. Vincent's. By 1860, it boasted a school, and by 1884 it also had a Roman Catholic church. The church and school served families with names like Halleran, St. Croix, Peddle, Butler, and Webber. Many of their descendants live in the area to this day.

If St. Vincent's is rich in history, it is also rich in stories. There are numerous tales about strange events, mysterious happenings, and, as might be expected, the odd ghost or two. As unlikely as it might sound, one of the most intriguing true ghost stories from the area starts with the discovery of an old pair of boots.

Boots are hardly frightening, one might think. Certainly there are no dark chapters in Newfoundland's history related to boots. Well, except perhaps the tale of the ill-fated Superior Rubber Company of the 1950s, with its obsolete German machinery and its over-budget (and often defective) footwear. But those skeletons in the post-Confederation closet aren't part of the horror story we are talking about here. No, just an ordinary, old pair of boots that turned out to be not quite so ordinary after all.

A number of years ago, there was a family with a number of daughters. This family lived quite close to the ocean at St. Vincent's.

Living so close to the ocean gave the girls plenty of opportunities to go beachcombing. Walking along the water's edge, they never knew what they might find. Certainly the sea offers up treasures every now and again, and if you look hard enough and long enough, you can find all kinds of wonderful things.

One day, the sisters were playing and exploring around the beach. Eventually, one of the older girls found a pair of very old boots that had obviously seen better days. Kids being what they are, the young girl thought they would be perfect for playing dress-up. So she packed up the boots and took her newfound treasure home.

Now, as any kid can tell you, moms have their own, very strange definitions of what is treasure and what is garbage. And as any mom can tell you, smelly old boots hauled up from the beach fall firmly into the second category. So, when the mother saw what had been discovered, she ordered her daughter to get rid of the malodorous things. The girl didn't listen, and just hid the boots in the porch.

As darkness fell, the woman got the children safely tucked into their beds for the night. But, as she was turning out the lights she discovered the old boots in the middle of the kitchen floor. Annoyed at not having been obeyed, she gave her daughter a bit of a lecture and threw the boots into the garbage.

Hours later, the peace of the night was broken by a strange noise. Everyone in the house was awakened by the sound of some-one coming up the stairs. The footsteps mounted the stairs slowly, step by step by step. Each footfall was accompanied by what seemed to be a wet, slushy sound. It sounded like a man walking in boots filled with water.

The mother told her children to stay in bed while she inves-tigated the disturbance, and left the room. Suddenly, the woman's screams rang through the house, and the family rushed to her side to see what was happening. Much to their horror, and right in front of them, was the source of the sloshing footsteps.

Somehow, the boots had escaped the imprisonment of the garbage can. But, as if this in itself were not enough, the boots were actually walking up the stairs before their very eyes!

Needless to say, the boots had to go. The mother and the daughter who had dragged the offending footwear home quickly put those boots into a bag and took them back to where they had been found. The boots were left on the beach at St. Vincent's, and they never bothered the family again.

It is one of those stories that certainly raises more questions than there are answers. Who was the ghostly owner of the mysterious boots? A fisherman lost at sea? A sailor swept from the deck of the Titanic? No one knows. But if you find a pair of old boots on the beach during your next trip to St. Vincent's, you might want to think twice before taking them home to mother.

THE TEAPOT
TABLE BAY, LABRADOR

OLD RUBBER BOOTS ARE NOT THE ONLY objects to get moved around by spirits. Table Bay, Labrador, has an interesting story concerning a ghost and a teapot.

Table Bay is located about thirty kilometres east of Cartwright. The place draws its name from a flat-topped local landmark, Table Hill, which is visible for some distance out to sea. The head of Table Bay formerly had a small year-round population, dating back as early as 1820. In 1856, the population was recorded at twenty-nine.

The south side of the bay was once dotted with winter houses at places such as Lugs Cove, Otter Brook, Burdett's Brook, Leddies (or Luddy's) Brook, Big Bight and Old Cove, and there were also several small fishing stations on the north side, including

Table Bay Point and Mullins Cove. According to D.W. Prowse's *History of Newfoundland*, Table Bay Point had the grand population of seven in 1891.

Historically, Table Bay was populated by families with names like Reeves, Macdonald, Pardy, Burdett, Heffler and Davis. In the twentieth century, the Davis family had a two-storey house in Table Bay that was possessed of a well-known reputation for being haunted.

The story of the Davis house was recorded for posterity in the pages of *Them Days* magazine in 1977, and from the account of the haunting, the house's ghosts were quite active. They were apparently fond of pulling chairs out from underneath people as they sat down, and were also quite a social lot, keeping visitors awake all night with the sound of ghostly talking in the kitchen.

While these activities are fairly common for phantoms, the Davis house was also home to some truly unusual paranormal activity. One winter, a couple by the name of Pardy were staying in the house while the Davis family wintered elsewhere.

One night, as Mrs. Pardy extinguished the lamp, the room was filled with a bright glowing light that shot across the floor like lightning. Much to the woman's amazement, the light was emanating from a rabbit bounding across the floor. The radiant rabbit hopped this way and that, then bolted across the room and vanished. When the hare disappeared, so did the light.

Another very strange event was witnessed by John Davis and Tommy Curl one night after brewing up a pot of tea in an old, big, blue enamel teapot. When they were finished, Curl straightened up for the night, while Davis put the teapot, still with a bit of tea in it, back on the top of the stove.

No more than five minutes later, Davis headed for the stairs to the upper storey. The staircase was constructed without a handrail, but with banister rails or spindles that went from each step straight up to the ceiling.

As he began to ascend the stairs, Davis was startled to meet the teapot coming down. Somehow, the pot had moved from the top of the stove to the top of the stairs. Exactly how it did this was something of a mystery. The two men were the only ones present, and the teapot itself was too large to fit between the spindles.

The teapot bounced down over the steps, clattering as it fell. When it reached the bottom of the staircase, the teapot struck the floor with a bang, and the remaining tea splattered over the door. Neither man could figure out how the teapot had transported itself from one place to another.

Try as they might, they could not get the tea stain off the door.

Eventually, the constant strange occurrences became too much for the Davis family. They dismantled the house completely, moved the pieces to nearby Leddies Brook, and rebuilt it as it had been before. After that, the family lived in the house for years, and were never troubled by ghosts again.

THE GHOST AND THE TOAST
ST. JOHN'S, AVALON PENINSULA

A HAUNTING INVOLVING A GRANDFATHER who refused to let death cut into his family time was experienced in St. John's in March of 1969. The grandfather in question had recently passed away, leaving to mourn his wife, along with her daughter, son-in-law and two-year-old grandson. All of them lived in the same house.

One morning, at about 6:00 A.M., the grandmother woke up and could smell toast. Checking to see if her grandson was still sleeping, she discovered that he was not in his bed. The house was quiet, and no one else had left their beds. Thinking that something might be burning in the kitchen, she went down to investigate.

When the woman reached the kitchen, she found her grandson eating toast at the kitchen table. The toaster itself was high up on a shelf, far out of reach of two-year-old hands. Surprised, she asked him how he had made the toast himself.

The young boy replied, "Nana, don't you know that Granddad got it for me?"

At first she thought he was joking, but then soon realized that there was no way he could have done it without the help of an adult. She woke her daughter and son-in-law, and asked them if they had made the grandchild the toast. They were as mystified as she.

THE MYSTERY OF
THE LOST LETTER
BISHOP'S FALLS, CENTRAL NEWFOUNDLAND

———

THE COMMUNITY OF BISHOP'S FALLS is one of those Newfoundland settlements which owes its development not to the fishery, but to the logging and paper industries. In 1901, Bishop's Falls had the whopping population of twenty. That changed in 1907 when a wood-pulp mill was established. The mill was completed and started producing pulp in 1911, and in the 1920s the mill and timber limits were sold to the Anglo-Newfoundland Development Company.

This was the start of new prosperity. In 1919, Bishop's Falls became the western headquarters for the activities of the Newfoundland Railway Company between the town and Port aux Basques. By 1967, the railway provided the second-biggest source of employment for the town.

It was around that time, thirty-five years ago, that a series of mysterious events was reported in a house in the community. The house in which the visitation took place still stands. Apparently its ghostly activity ceased many years ago. Nonetheless, it remains a remarkable account of the paranormal, and one which remains of interest even though many years have passed.

The woman who told me the story was only seven years old when her family moved into a two- storey house in Bishop's Falls, sometime around 1965. She lived there from the ages of seven to eleven, and to this day remains fascinated by the events that took place there.

The front door to the family's house opened onto a stairway which led to the upper floor. The upper storey had four bedrooms, one on either side of the staircase and two at the other end of a hall. The story that went with the house was that an old man, a previous occupant, had died there and that the room at the end of the hall had been his bedroom.

It was this room that was the focal point of the house's haunting. The other three rooms on the upper storey were also bedrooms, but the "ghost's bedroom" was never used as such. The room was very plain, and had a simple old door with a distinctive squeak when it was swung open.

Not long after the family moved into the house, they began to hear the sounds of the front door of the house opening, followed by the noise of footsteps climbing the staircase. The footsteps would continue down the hall, and would then be joined by the squeak of the door opening. This happened many times in the four years the family lived there.

On one occasion, the family's grandmother stayed at the house for the night, sharing a bed with her granddaughter. She too heard the same noises and footsteps, but she also experienced a far more intense visitation. She had listened to the footsteps drawing closer down the hall, but instead of continuing on to the rear of the house, they paused just outside her door.

After a brief pause, the eerie steps continued into the room. Next, the woman could feel the coldness of the air play against her as the sheets rose. This was not the end of the event, however, as she then felt the sensation of the bed settling down as if the weight of another body had been added to it.

The grandmother had known the gentleman who had died there, and she swore that he had climbed into the bed at her feet. It is the sort of event that might make you think twice about complaining about your partner's cold feet in the middle of the night. After all, the freezing feet of someone you love are probably far better than the deathly cold digits of someone, or something, you have never met before.

The grandmother was not the only visiting family member to come face to face (or toe to toe, as the case may be) with the spirit. One evening, an uncle was babysitting. It was quite late when the parents returned. Rather than journey back to his own house, he decided to spend the night.

In the middle of the night, the uncle leaped from his bed and hurried home rather than stay in the dwelling another second. He refused to ever spend another night there, and also refused to describe exactly what he had experienced. Reportedly, from that point on he always felt quite uncomfortable in the building, even when visiting in the bright light of day.

The house itself had an apartment. This apartment was joined to the main house along the rear wall, up against the unused room. The tenant in the apartment would call from time to time, sometimes in the middle of night, waking the family. The tenant would then complain of noises disturbing her sleeping children, swearing that there must be a party going on to produce such noise. The occupants of the main section of the house had heard no such noises.

Other than annoying neighbours and terrifying uncles, the ghost never caused any damage or really bothered anyone too much. But the fact he was around at all was enough to be disturbing.

Eventually, the mother of the family decided that it was pointless to have an unused room in the house. After she made up her mind to renovate the empty room at the back of the house, she started to strip the walls. It was during this renovation that a letter was discovered sealed up in the wall. The woman brought the letter to the landlord and related the story of its discovery.

From that day forward, the noises stopped. The family came to the conclusion that the ghost of the former resident had been coming home searching for the letter, and that when it was uncovered, his spirit had been released from the house.

There may be some precedents to their theory. In many reported cases of hauntings, there is the idea of unfinished business. This unresolved business may be something major, but paranormal researcher Hans Holzer has argued in his book *Ghosts: True Encounters with the World Beyond* that it may be something quite minor. Drawing on decades of research into ghost sightings, he goes on to state that it may even be as minor as not having answered a couple of letters!

The contents of the letter found in the empty room in Bishop's Falls remain a mystery, and one that may never be resolved. But it is interesting to think that there may be other ghosts out there, still wandering the earth because of letters unwritten or undelivered during their lifetime.

A VACANT LOT WITH A GHOSTLY PAST
QUEEN'S ROAD, ST. JOHN'S

THE VACANT LOT LOCATED TO THE WEST of the Theatre Pharmacy on Queen's Road was not always vacant. From the 1890s up to the mid-1980s, it was the location of a three-storey row house.

In March of 1974, a family moved into that house. With their first steps into the house, they became possessed by an eerie, uncomfortable feeling. There was nothing to account for the oppressive feelings, except perhaps the faint scratching noises coming from inside the walls which permeated the house once darkness fell.

Before long, they discovered that the white stone step outside the back door was inscribed with lettering. Brushing off the dirt, it became apparent that the stone was an old tombstone, removed from hallowed ground. The eerie feelings continued and deepened. Members of the family began to spend more than a few nights at neighbours'. They started to feel encompassed by the house, as if the house itself was staring at them, watching them at all times.

One son woke in the middle of the night and saw a male figure. Thinking it was his brother, and only half awake, the boy watched the figure walk toward toward the bed as he drifted back to sleep. When he woke, he found that his clothes had been moved around the room. His brother denied any involvement and, indeed, denied being in the room that night at all.

The intensity of the visitations increased. One night, three members of the family watched a glowing orb of red light appear at the bottom of the staircase. Suspended in mid-air, it began to dance back and forth, moving up and down the banister.

A friend of the family visited, only to feel hands on her shoulders and to hear a moaning when she came in the front door. One of the brothers had someone grab him by the shoulder one day when he was home alone. Later that same day, he fell asleep on the chesterfield in the parlour, and awoke to a terrifying sight. There, in the middle of the room, an open grave had materialized, a hole through the floor, dug into the earth beneath the house. It was no dream. The terrifying, yawning grave was so real that the young man had to step over it to get out of the room. When he returned with help, it was gone.

Spiritual assistance was requested, and a Roman Catholic priest arrived with holy water to bless the first floor. When he got to the second floor, he hurried his steps. When he got up to the third, he disappeared into an unused room at the back of the house. He emerged immediately and fled the building. The only words he spoke to the family before departing were, "I would advise you to leave."

The family had lived in the premises for four months. They were fated to live there no longer, for one night shortly after the priest's chilling admonition, in the exact words of one eyewitness, "all hell broke loose."

One son woke, knowing something was wrong. He came downstairs to find his entire family awake and his mother frantic. In the front hall there was a wooden hatch set into the floor, leading to a dirt-floored crawl space beneath the house. The hatch was lifting and banging shut repeatedly. When it did stop, all the doors upstairs banged open and shut. Accompanying this din was the sound of beating on the walls. The unholy racket continued all night, and stopped with the advent of daylight. The family left and never returned.

An uncle heard about this, ridiculed their superstitious natures, and moved in. Where his relatives had lasted four months, he lasted only one, deciding to leave after he woke up one morning to find nail marks going from his neck all the way down his spine, as if clawed hands had scratched all the way down his back while he slept.

The building itself was demolished by 1984, but the vacant lot it left behind is still charged with a hellish energy, and recently was the location of a gruesome and as of yet unresolved murder case. Today, twenty-eight years since he lived there, one of the surviving family members is still tortured by nightmares, and to this day dreams of standing in front of the house, looking up, and finding someone watching him from the top window.

THE GHOST TRAIN

BUCHANS, CENTRAL NEWFOUNDLAND

CONSTRUCTION ON THE FIRST RAIL LINE in Newfoundland began in August 1881. By January of 1882, the province's first train ran on an experimental basis from St. John's to Donovans. By summer, there were regular excursions to Conception Bay, and by fall the line had reached Holyrood.

Over the years, rail lines spread across the Island, a number of which were operated by private corporations. The Anglo-Newfoundland Development Company had several lines at different times. Others were operated by Price Newfoundland, Bowater's, the Newfoundland Iron Ore Company, and the Dominion Iron and Steel Company.

In its heyday, the Buchans rail line was home to a phantom locomotive which only appeared when a worker had died. (Courtesy of Karen Moore)

The proliferation of rail lines across the Newfoundland and Labrador landscape meant that the trains and the tracks entered into the cultural life and folklore of the people. It was not long, for example, that ghost stories began to spring up connected to the railway.

There are a number of ghost stories from across the province which involve the rail system in one way or another. One of the most intriguing ghost stories of this genre was passed on to me by Margaret (Peg) Moore. Today, Peg lives in Mount Pearl, but she is full of stories about her native town, the community of Buchans. Peg was born and raised in Buchans, and lived there for the first sixteen years of her life. Peg's father, Dan Beresford, worked for the Buchans mining company for a total of forty-eight and a half years.

Peg recalls a story she heard when she was growing up in Buchans about a phantom train which was said to appear on the company rail line built by the American Smelting and Refining Company (ASARCO).

The rail line was all part of a large-scale mining operation run by ASARCO. In 1906, a Mi'kmaq woodsman by the name of Matty Mitchell had discovered rich ore bodies in the bed of the Buchans River. By 1915, ASARCO had learned about the copper, lead and zinc, and organized experiments to separate the metals. They were successful in 1925. In 1928, a thirty-five- kilometre (twenty-two miles) rail line was built by ASARCO to carry ore concentrate from the mines in Buchans to Millertown, where the main railway took it to Botwood.

Work on the line was not always easy or safe, and there were a number of accidents on the Buchans train, and a number of company workers died over the years along the tracks.

It was after one of those accidents that the ghost train would make an appearance. The train would be steaming toward Millertown, when the crew or passengers would look ahead and see a light approaching them. As the light grew closer, it would appear as if a second train were steaming along the tracks, heading direct-ly toward the first train. Just when collision seemed inevitable, the mystery train would disappear completely.

In July 1977, the final load of ore was sent on the railway to Millertown and then to Botwood. Then, like the remainder of the rail lines on the island portion of the province, the Buchans line vanished. With the trains no longer running, there is no chance of further accidents on the line, and consequently, our chances of see-ing the infamous phantom train of Buchans have vanished as well.

CHAPTER 6

The Final Curtain:
Murders, Deaths, and
Other Strange Undertakings

A MATTER OF MURDER
QUEEN'S ROAD, ST. JOHN'S

O_{NE} OF THE OLDEST RECORDED STORIES of a haunting in St. John's dates to the year 1745. It involves one Samuel Pettyham, a St. John's man who rented a small house on the fringe area of town. The man found a housekeeper to come in during the days to cook and clean, and who would then leave at night. The woman expressed some concern about him remaining alone in the house at night, but he dismissed her worries.

Soon after moving in, Pettyham was awake late one night, reading a book in the kitchen by lamplight. He was just about to put away the book, when he thought he heard the click of the door latch on the back door. Suddenly, he saw the door latch lift and then slowly fall back into place. The lock to the door was bolted, and the door didn't open.

Fearing burglars, Pettyham rushed to the front of the house and bolted the lock. No sooner had he done this than that latch too began to rise. There was a momentary hesitation, and then slowly the latch dropped back down into place. He was determined to see who was outside the door, unbolted it and threw the door open wide. There was no one there.

As the weeks wore on, the same lifting of the latches was repeated, always without any sign of a human culprit. Close to a month later, Pettyham had all the proof he needed that the lifting had an unearthly origin.

Pettyham had been visiting a friend in the west end of town. As it was late, his host offered to drive Pettyham home in his carriage. As the horse drew near to the laneway to the house, it stopped suddenly, and refused to move an inch farther forward.

Pettyham offered to walk the rest of the way. As he walked along, he saw in front of him a glowing light. Thinking it was from a lantern or light of some kind carried by another person, Pettyham quickened his step.

About twenty yards farther on, the figure stepped out into the moonlight in front of Pettyham's house. The figure stood perfectly erect for one moment, and then turned and faced Pettyham, who took one look and turned and fled in absolute horror. The figure he had seen was that of a very tall man, a man with his head cut completely off, close to the shoulders.

Pettyham raced back up along Queen's Road, burst into a boarding house and begged for shelter for the night. After he calmed down, he gave a clear description of the event, and was told a most miraculous tale.

The headless man he had seen was the spectre of a well-known captain of a ship that plied its trade between England and Newfoundland. The captain had been the companion of a beautiful lady, who dwelt within the house later occupied by Pettyham. Whenever the captain was in St. John's, the two were always seen together. But while he was out to sea, she showered her affections on a local man.

Apparently the captain's nearness to the lady was too much for the local man, who decided to do away with his competition. One night, just as the captain said goodbye to the lady, the jealous lover leaped forward with an exceptionally sharp sword and removed the captain's head.

The man who committed the deed was never convicted, although all signs of guilt seemed to point to him. The soul of the headless captain, it is believed, still wanders, doomed to search eternally for his unpunished murderer.

THE SHADOW WOMAN
PATRICK STREET, ST. JOHN'S

In the summer of 1969, a woman was walking up Patrick Street in the west end of St. John's, on her way home from a friend's house. It was just getting dark. At that time, the stuccoed house on the corner of Patrick and Power Streets was vacant and a FOR SALE sign stood out front. As she passed, something made her turn around and look up at the second-floor window.

There was a shadow of a woman in the window, looking like the sort of shadow that might be produced by a person standing in front of a lamp. The woman was brushing her hair. The woman on the street stood transfixed, watching for a few moments. As she watched, it dawned on her that there was no light in the room and there was no one living in the house.

The woman walked past that house many times afterwards, but never again saw the ghost. Later, neighbourhood people informed her that the house is reportedly haunted by the ghost of a woman who was killed within.

A close neighbour living on Patrick Street also witnessed a number of events that made her head turn. There was a figure that appeared half a dozen times. The first time she saw it, she took it for the man who lived there. She waved, but there was no response. The drape fell across the window, and it was not until later that she realized that no one was home. Even later, that woman was told the story of the murder which had occurred in the house. From that point on, she made a point of waving at the window every time she passed by, hoping that her kindness would give the ghostly woman some peace in her unrest.

A DUEL TO THE DEATH
PRINGLE PLACE, ST. JOHN'S

O N A SNOWY EVENING IN MARCH, 1826, Ensign Philpot of the Royal Navy and a Captain Rudkin of the British Army were gambling with cards at Fort Townshend. As the night wore on, Philpot lost more and more. The other players drifted away till it was only Rudkin and Philpot left. At the last game, Rudkin dealt the final hand, and Philpot lost.

As Rudkin reached for the cash, Philpot grabbed for it. Rudkin took the money back, forcibly, and started to leave the room. As he did so, Philpot threw a mug of water at the captain, and kicked him from behind. Gravely insulted, Rudkin took the only honourable course of action left open to him, and challenged Philpot to a duel.

The two foes met March 30, and despite the entreaties of their seconds, each was determined to see the other firmly in hell. The order was given to fire. The ensign, shooting into the light of the cruel sun, missed completely. The captain, it is reported, leapt into the air, firing wildly. The bullet from his pistol impacted squarely on Philpot's chest, killing him on the spot.

The mortal remains of Ensign John Philpot, aged twenty-seven, were buried in the Anglican churchyard on April Fool's Day, and duly recorded in the Cathedral's Register of Burials. But Philpot did not rest easily in his grave. Soon after his burial, the shadowy figure of a young officer began to haunt the place of his death, a figure witnessed by many sober townspeople. Even horses passing the spot are said to have shied away, inexplicably.

During the construction of the Anglican Cathedral, the remains of an officer were exhumed, remains thought to belong to unfortunate Philpot. Denied revenge and a secure resting place, his soul seems doomed to wander for eternity.

SIMPSON'S TAVERN
DOWNTOWN AREA, ST. JOHN'S

BEFORE THE TURN OF THE TWENTIETH CENTURY, there was said to be in St. John's a public house known as Simpson's Tavern. Because of its rather sinister reputation, it was known from one end of town to the other. The tavern was known to be haunted by the spirit of a young girl who had been murdered in the alleyway behind the tavern. Far from being a passive spirit, the ghost was known to be vengeful and destructive.

The ghost's actions reached a horrific pinnacle with an event concerning a man named O'Hare. O'Hare was known to be a thoroughly disreputable character in his own right, with a rumoured record of child molestation. One night, O'Hare told his fellow drinkers in Simpson's tavern that he had noticed a young girl in the back alley, and that he was going to go talk with her.

O'Hare staggered drunkenly out of the door and down along the dark alley. He was only gone a matter of minutes when a terrifying scream shook the patrons of the public house. Seizing lanterns, they rushed into the alley, and were confronted by an ungodly sight.

There on the filthy ground, dying from a massive wound to the throat, lay O'Hare, great gouts of blood pouring out on the stones. Above him, like the angel of death, hovered the figure of a little girl, licking her blood-stained lips. For one brief moment she remained, glowering at the crowd, and then vanished, leaving them alone in the alley with the drained corpse of O'Hare.

THE GHASTLY TRIO
QUEEN'S ROAD, ST. JOHN'S

THE AREA NEAR THE INTERSECTION of Long's Hill and Queen's Road was once the staging site for St. John's finest cockfights. It is also something of a magnet for noteworthy paranormal activity. But by far the most intriguing haunting in this area is that of 92 Queen's Road, today a pale-yellow three-storey house. Ninety-two Queen's Road is the haunt of a chilling ghostly trio, a trio made only more terrifying by the history of the property itself.

A number of years ago, the top floor of the house was occupied by a family, with the second floor being occupied by the family's grandmother. Now, the grandmother was up in years and often complained of the sound of babies crying upstairs, the sound of two infants crying when there were no babies in the building. The woman would also tell her grandchildren stories of watching a woman slowly climb the stairs to the upper apartment.

The family humoured her and dismissed her stories as the rambling of an elderly woman. This, however, did not deter the grandmother, who went on and on about the crying babies and the mysterious woman.

Years later, the truth of the building's dark history was revealed. You see, 92 Queen's Road was the focal point for one of the most sensational, and unsolved, murder cases of the 1950s. In 1957, three teenaged boys made a gruesome discovery just outside the city limits of St. John's.

The boys found what they thought was a bundle, with what seemed to be an arm protruding from it, covered with blood. One of the boys thought it was a dog, and kicked at it, revealing that is was in fact the corpse of an infant human child, and that the corpse had been burned.

The police were summoned, and the subsequent search revealed not one, but two corpses. The first was burned considerably, and covered with charred papers, tissue, and bits of clothing. The second body was in a decomposed state and had been dead for some time, though it was tidily dressed in a nightgown with handiwork around the throat. The second corpse was almost mummified, flattened to a thickness of about three inches, and dried and hard like a piece of board.

The discovery of the bodies made headlines overnight. On the testimony of a local taxi driver, the police quickly arrested a thirty-seven-year-old woman living at 92 Queen's Road. The taxi driver claimed to have picked up the woman and taken her to the area where the babies were later found, and had waited while the woman burned a box of what she claimed contained old clothes, and then had driven her home. The woman was charged with the illegal disposal of a human corpse.

The court case that followed was full of unanswered questions. The accused proved she was not the mother of the babies, as she had not given birth in several years. Furthermore, she denied ever having seen the babies and claimed not to have been picked up by the taxi driver. The cabman stuck to his story of taking her to the site. The accused was found with large sums of cash on her person at the time of her arrest, cash which she refused to explain. In the end, the accused was found not guilty. It is written that she thanked her lawyer, tossed her hair back and smiled at the police officers as she left the room.

The trial was over, but the crime was not solved. Two babies had been murdered, their innocent, lily-white bodies mutilated, and to this date no one has ever been charged. Memory of the incident has faded, and today, the only reminders of the case come from beyond the grave... the shadowy figure of an unknown woman climbing the stairs of 92 Queen's Road, and the faint sounds of unseen babies crying out, crying out in fear perhaps at the approach of their ghostly murderess.

BODIES IN BARRELS
ST. LAWRENCE, BURIN PENINSULA

AROUND 1835, ONE OF THE ENGLISH clerks at the Newman and Company's plantation in St. Lawrence on the Burin Peninsula suffered a rather untimely demise. Embalming of any sort was an impossibility in that far-flung fishing station, so the unfortunate man's body was preserved inside a puncheon of rum until the body, by that point well pickled, could be taken back to Europe for burial. While unusual perhaps by today's standards, this practice was apparently not uncommon.

The most famous of these pickled corpses was Admiral Horatio Nelson, who himself had a Newfoundland connection. In May of 1782, Nelson, in command of the HMS *Abbemarie*, spent several days in St. John's. Nelson was not impressed with St. John's, and in a letter home to England described it as a most disagreeable place. During his stay, he spent most of his time courting the bottle at the historic Ship Inn, close to what is now the Crow's Nest on Water Street.

Thankfully, the Admiral turned down a post in Provincial Tourism, and left St. John's. In true heroic fashion, he was killed at the Battle of Trafalgar in 1805, and was shipped back to England in a barrel of brandy. According to naval legend, when the barrel was finally opened, it was found to be drained of its liquor. Apparently, sailors unaware of the true contents had tapped it for some illicit tippling.

These tales have a gruesome similarity to another story from the community of St. Lawrence, which apparently had a strange association with disturbing objects inside casks. The event in question shocked the community when the preserved corpse of an African baby was found sealed up inside a puncheon of molasses which had been imported from the West Indies.

... AND IN BOXES ...
DOWNTOWN AREA, ST. JOHN'S

THE DELIGHT OF FINDING A BODY sealed up inside a container of one sort or another is reflected in a popular ghost story from downtown St. John's. Sometime around the 1870s, a married couple by the name of Packerson moved into St. John's from a settlement in Conception Bay, and rented the house for two pounds, four shillings a month. Mrs. Packerson always felt that she was being followed through the house, and this made her feel very uneasy.

The months slipped by, and Mr. Packerson was offered a berth on a sailing vessel. It was barely a week after his departure when his wife had the horrifying experience of coming face to face with the house's paranormal inhabitant. On that day, Mrs. Packerson had three times attempted to light the gas burner in the kitchen, and three times someone beside her blew out the flame. In a state of frenzy, she turned to run from the kitchen but she was unable to move one inch.

Directly in front of her, in what she was using as a closet, she saw the figure of a woman standing in the doorway, illuminated with a dazzling brightness from the crown of her head to the very soles of her feet. Mrs. Packerson stared at the amazing spectacle for a few moments before realizing that she was actually gazing upon the figure of a ghost. When she realized what she was witnessing, she instinctively put her hands to her eyes, and fell into a state of unconsciousness.

When she revived, she ran to her neighbours, who informed her that a former owner had killed his wife, placed her body in a box, walled it up inside the closet, and had fled the country before the murder was uncovered. By the time the Packersons entered the story, they had been able to rent the house so cheaply only because the place was known to be haunted by the unhappy spectre of the murdered bride.

BURIED ALIVE!
HARBOURFRONT, ST. JOHN'S

IN THE EARLY HALF OF THE NINETEENTH CENTURY, the St. John's harbourfront was a much more dangerous place than it is now. The harbour was thick with foreign vessels, the wharves treacherous with fat and oil, and rum cost a penny a glass. Needless to say, many an unknown body was found in the wee hours of the morning, floating face down in the dark waters of the harbour. The city at that point had no morgue, and the Government paid a standing salary to a Nancy Coyle to prepare unclaimed corpses for burial. Her house became a temporary resting spot for bodies bound for the boneyard.

Once, as fair Nancy was driving the final nails into his coffin, a Dutch sailor revived in time to prevent himself from being buried alive. While Nancy is said to have brought many a corpse back to

The St. John's harbourfront, shown here in the late nineteenth century, was once a much more dangerous place than it is today. (Courtesy of the City of St. John's Archives)

life, one is left wondering how many unconscious mariners were not as fortunate as the nameless Dutchman.

BELL STREET GHOST
BELL STREET, ST. JOHN'S

————

Eᴍᴘᴛʏ ᴛᴏᴅᴀʏ, ʙᴇʟʟ sᴛʀᴇᴇᴛ ɪs ꜰᴏᴜɴᴅ off Duckworth Street in downtown St. John's. This area was the site of St. John's first Pentecostal mission, the first Jewish Synagogue, and the first Temperance Hall, all of which were destroyed in the Great St. John's Fire of 1892. The neighbourhood was rebuilt from the ashes, only to be slowly worn down once more through a series of demolitions and smaller fires, such as that which destroyed the home of Thomas Downey, early in the morning of July 21, 1924. It spread with such rapidity that the inhabitants saved nothing, while neighbours were forced to run from their houses in their nightclothes.

The last house on Bell Street was conveniently bulldozed to make room for parking just a few short years ago.

This neighbourhood was also, as is typical for that area of St. John's, haunted. The haunting took place in one of the residential buildings that was constructed along the street in the years following the Great St. John's Fire of 1892. In the early part of the twentieth century, the house in question apparently had quite a well-known local reputation as a haunted dwelling, and as a result, it was difficult to keep tenants in the building. At one point, the house was occupied by a woman who had a particularly vivid encounter with the local spirit.

The woman awoke one night to find that she was not alone in her bedroom. There, standing at the end of her bed, was a glowing-white spectral figure. The apparition had the appearance of a corpse wrapped up in a traditional, white winding sheet, which was once a common burial custom in Newfoundland. The figure stood, arms crossed over its chest, as silent as the grave.

Sadly, the spirit of Bell Street seems to have vanished along with the houses which once lined the street, as it has not been seen for several generations.

COAKER MONUMENT
PORT UNION, TRINITY BAY

———

An odd phenomenon has been reported at the William Coaker monument in the historic community of Port Union. According to some accounts, on days when not the slightest breeze is blowing, a

An eerie breeze has been reported at the William F. Coaker monument in Port Union, Trinity Bay. (Courtesy of the Heritage Foundation of Newfoundland and Labrador)

sudden gusty wind has been known to spring up on entry through the gates to the monument site, a wind which can be felt on one side of the gates, but not on the other.

Now, it seems that every other cove in Newfoundland is haunted by the ghost of someone or other who died at sea. Perhaps the monument's ghostly breeze is nothing less than the spirit of Sir William F. Coaker himself, organizing all those phantom fishermen and spectral sealers to fight for better haunting conditions in the afterlife. After all, the "Fishermen's Paranormal Union" has a nice ring to it, doesn't it?

GRAVEYARD GHOSTS
HOLYROOD, CONCEPTION BAY

HOLYROOD SITS AT THE HEAD of Conception Bay, spread out along the shoreline of a deep, well-protected inlet known as Holyrood Bay. For over a hundred years, the community has been known as a tourism and recreation destination, a tradition that continues today with its restaurants, shops and marina.

Although local tradition maintains that Holyrood's first settlers arrived in the late 1600s, historical evidence suggests that the first permanent settlers arrived between 1770 and the 1790s. While most of them were Irish, folklore states that a small number of Mi'kmaq from Placentia Bay and a handful of Portuguese also made Holyrood their new home.

From the early 1830s onward, Holyrood has been the link between Conception Bay and the communities of Placentia Bay via the Salmonier Line. In 1835, Deputy Government Surveyor Josiah Blackburn was commissioned to make a preliminary survey of a road to be laid out between Holyrood and Salmonier, and work was begun shortly thereafter. In 1859, the House of Assembly voted to allocate £250 to improve the condition of the roadway.

Toward the end of the 1800s, one enterprising man by the name of William established a wagon business to haul goods and

people to and from Holyrood along Salmonier Line. William invest-
ed in a particularly fine horse, strong and healthy, which he had
imported from Canada for the purpose of hauling the wagon and its
freight.

One night, on his way back into the North Arm section of
Holyrood, the wagon driver and his beast of burden underwent
a terrifying ordeal. The path that William had chosen took the
wagon through the middle of an old graveyard. As the wagon
clattered and clacked along the road, a strange noise was
heard. It sounded as if the wagon was going over a wooden
bridge, the wheels making the distinctive noise of rolling over
wooden planks. As this happened, the horse stopped dead in its
tracks.

It was a dark evening, and was around midnight. When the
horse stopped, Will got down off the driver's seat to investigate. As
he jumped down from the cart, Will's leather boots crunched
against the gravel of the path. At this sound, he knew that there
was no wooden bridge underneath them.

Will stood in the darkness beside his horse. The wind blew
through the graveyard, whistling around the tombstones. Much to
his horror, the wind was joined by another sound. The clamour of
voices, all jumbled together like the unintelligible din of a crowd,
began to emanate from the graves on all sides. This noise grew
louder, and closer, and then was combined with the sound of people climbing onto the wagon. The wagon rattled and creaked and
then grew silent, as if the invisible throng was waiting for their
ride to begin.

White-faced, Will decided that they had already dallied too
long in the boneyard. He slapped the horse on its hindquarters, and
urged it to move along and out of the vicinity of the strange noises. The horse obliged, and started forward. The creature leaned into
its yoke, straining against an invisible weight. The wagon creaked
to life once more, and started to move.

The horse pulled, hard. Will walked alongside as the horse strained harder and harder. Every so often, the driver looked back in fear at the empty wagon. The beast soldiered on, but it acted as if the weight of the wagon was immense. It would move forward along the dark road only about two wagon lengths before it would stop, drained of energy. Its owner urged it forward again, and the horse would drag itself forward another short distance before grinding to a halt once more.

The horse travelled very slowly under the heavy, ghostly load. Suddenly, the wagon lurched forward with a tremendous jerking motion, as if its intangible passengers had leapt off all at once.

With the weight of the wagon returned to normal, the horse plodded on a little farther, but then gradually slowed, dead tired, and unable to pull any more. Taking pity on the horse, and not wishing to remain out of doors any longer than was necessary, William unhitched the horse. He left the wagon behind and started off, leading the horse by the bridle.

Will led the animal down Vatch's Hill to a property he knew. He hoped that he would find someone at home, and that he would be allowed to stable his horse in the barn for the night. Unfortunately, no one was to be found, so Will started the long walk around the head of the bay, back to his own house.

By the time the weary coachman got home, it was very late. The horse looked in poor shape, and by the time it was placed into its own barn, it was two o'clock in the morning. Too tired to do much more, Will went into the family house, woke his father, and asked the father to go feed the exhausted animal.

Will's father went out to feed the horse, but soon came back wearing a puzzled expression. He asked Will what had happened to the horse, as the beast refused to eat the oats which had been offered. Dragging himself from the warmth and comfort of his bed, Will went back outside to check on the horse.

The father had been correct. The horse refused to eat, and simply stood there in its stall, breathing heavily, overcome with the events of the night. William waited by the side of the horse, stroking its mane and talking to it in a soothing voice. Several hours later, at around five o'clock, the horse sank down to its knees, gave a great heaving breath, and died.

There are many stories from across the province of horses being sensitive to beings from the netherworld. On the west coast of the Island, stories circulate around the Port au Port region about horses which could see ghosts, and which refused to walk along paths the ghosts frequented.

Holyrood, however, has something of a unique and disturbing claim. While other parts of the province may have had horses which could see supernatural beings, Holyrood may have the only story of a horse that met its untimely end due to paranormal interference.

THE MURDERED PIPER
SWIFT CURRENT, PLACENTIA BAY

THE COMMUNITY OF SWIFT CURRENT is located on "The Heritage Run," twenty-one kilometres from the Trans-Canada Highway. The earliest settlers in the area were named Pike, Darby, Brown, and Pine, mostly of Irish descent. Originally, the settlement was known as Piper's Hole, and its first inhabitants arrived to hunt, trap, and fish for salmon in the mid-eighteenth century. Another early industry was the cutting of timber, and a nearby settlement named Black River was the location of the first pulp mill in Newfoundland.

Today, the Swift Current/Piper's Hole River area is a favourite spot for vacationers. Just down the road is Piper's Hole River Provincial Park which contains a scheduled salmon river, making it a spot well known to the anglers of the province.

Lucky visitors, however, might be treated to something more than beautiful scenery and good fishing. It is said that if the breeze is just right, you might hear the sound of a ghostly piper, his spirit playing to the wind.

The ghostly piper has been playing his instrument for centuries, and his playing gave the location its name. According to some, the phantom musician was a piper in the French army in the eighteenth century. In this version of the legend, the French and English clashed in battle at a spot nearby called Garden Cove. Supposedly, the spirit of the French soldier lingers in the river valley, mournfully playing a pipe. If this version of the legend is true, the French piper was probably playing an instrument more like a fife than a set of bagpipes.

There are some, however, who say that the ghostly piper does play bagpipes. They add that the piper is not French, but Scottish. Their version of the tale has even been immortalized and promoted on the Town of Swift Current's community access Web site!

In the late seventeenth and early eighteenth centuries, fishing boats would come to Newfoundland from Europe every summer to fish. One particular ship carried a crew of Englishmen and one Scottish gentleman by the name of Kelly. Kelly, true to the stereotype of Scots worldwide, loved to play the bagpipes, and would often play for the men on the ship in the evenings.

When the weather was bad for fishing, the crew would ofttimes go ashore to hunt for game and to explore the coast. One such windy and stormy day, Kelly and a fellow crewman, an Englishman named Morrisey, set off on a hunting expedition.

In a terrible hunting accident, Morrisey shot Kelly. He found to his horror that the piper had been killed instantly. Morrisey was aghast at what he had done, and panic-stricken, the guilty man disposed of the body in a nearby pond. In his terror, he did not notice the growing storm.

The weather grew rougher and rougher, and by the time Morrisey returned to the shoreline, it was too stormy to reach the ship moored offshore. The guilt-ridden man was forced instead to spent three torturous nights in a wet cave before he was able to return to the vessel. Upon rejoining his companions, the ill-fated hunter told the crew that somehow he and Kelly had been separated in the storm.

The captain of the fishing vessel sent ashore a search party to look for the missing man. Not surprisingly, they failed to locate Kelly and assumed that he was either killed by the local Beothuk, or that he had died of exposure during the tempest. The ship weighed anchor, and sailed back to Europe. From that day on, ghostly music could be heard every day at dusk near the spot where the piper had been killed.

At this point, the story takes a turn that seems even more fantastic, and which may be a modern addition to an old legend. Apparently, many years later, the music stopped just as mysteriously as it started.

The night the piping stopped in Newfoundland, an aged sailor named Morrisey died in England. On his deathbed, the old man confessed to a young priest of a terrible crime he had committed years ago far over the sea in Newfoundland. The young priest blessed the man, and he passed on to his great reward.

Years went by. Eventually, and by remarkable coincidence, the priest was sent to minister in Newfoundland not far from Piper's Hole. Once he had lived there a while, the local residents told the priest the story of the eerie pipe music. The priest remembered the confession of the old sailor. In amazement, he realized that he had given last rites to the murderer responsible for the Piper's Hole ghost.

Like many Newfoundland and Labrador legends, the exact historical origins of the tale will probably never be known with any great certainty. While the confession of the aged Morrisey may be a more recent addition to the story, either one of the two versions of the piper's death could contain a grain of truth.

But was the piper French or Scottish? If you believe the first version, the version involving the death of the French army piper, there is a chance he could have been either.

As noted earlier, he could have been a French piper, one of the soldiers who relayed orders using a fife or similar instrument to soldiers farther down the line. In the 1700s, however, the time when the battle was said to occur, numerous Jacobite Scots did fight in French uniform for the French Army, and may have had their own bagpiper with them.

Perhaps the French piper was in fact a Scottish piper after all, and the myth of Morrisey and Kelly grew up around the core of the tale as it was passed down through the generations. Like Kelly's hidden body, the truth will probably never be found. Next time you are visiting Swift Current, however, take a walk at dusk and keep your ears alert for the mysterious music of Piper's Hole.

BITTER ANN POWER
BITTER ANN'S COVE, PLACENTIA BAY

NOT FAR FROM PIPER'S HOLE is one of the more intriguing place names in Newfoundland. Bitter Ann's Cove is located east of Garden Cove, near the head of Placentia Bay. The origin of the name has a dramatic story associated with it, which also incorporates a ghost story.

According to authors and kayaking aficionados Kevin Redmond and Dan Murphy, the cove is named after a woman by the name of Ann Power. Ann and her husband John Power moved to the cove one winter in the early 1800s. John had been drawn to the cove due to the rich timber grounds. It was his plan to spend the winter cutting lumber for use the following year.

Everything went smoothly as the couple settled into their new winter home. As the year drew to a close, the isolation began to wear on the couple, particularly John. John's sister was expecting a child, and as the Christmas season fell upon them, John's desire to see his family grew.

Eventually, John decided that he had to leave the cove to make a day trip to call upon his family. Ann stayed behind to mind their house, and John promised her he would be home soon. Before he left, the woodcutter said to his wife, "If I am a living man, I'll be home tonight."

John's sister was living on Bar Haven Island, situated on the northern part of the west side of Placentia Bay. By the1830s, around the time of John's visit, the island was quite populous, boasting a population of 130, a Justice of the Peace, a constable, school and church.

The brother arrived safely, and was warmly received by his sister. Whether it was the reunion that was cause for some celebration, or whether it was simply the nature of the festive holiday season, John made merry. As he did, the weather started to turn ugly.

Before long, a blizzard was raging. His good judgement clouded by one too many glasses of rum, John decided that he would set out. He buttoned up his coat, and set off in his small boat back toward the cove.

In the cove, Ann stared out into the growing blizzard, fearful for her husband's safety. She left the house and went out into the storm, hoping to catch a glimpse of John's boat. There was no sign of him. She returned to the house to warm herself, and then went out a second time. She could see no boat.

The wind howled, and the snow continued to fall. Hours passed, and sick with worry, Ann went out a third time to search for her missing husband. She fought her way down to the seashore, and nearing the strand, tripped against an object half buried in the snow.

Brushing the snow aside, she discovered with mounting horror that she had tripped over John's frozen corpse.

John had been close to the cove when his boat had overturned in the waves. The boat was quickly lost in the blizzard. The man fought his way to shore, but his immersion in the frigid December waters was too much for his system. Hypothermia overtook him, and he froze to death before reaching the warmth and safety of his house.

Ann found herself stranded in the cove, without a boat and with no way of contacting another soul. She was lost and beside herself, without a clue of what to do.

Just when things seemed hopeless, the spirit of her dead mother appeared before her. The helpful ghost gave instructions on how to prepare John's corpse for burial. The spectre then offered the following words of advice, saying,

"Go to the point, light a fire and stay there."

The ghost then faded away.

Not one to argue with a ghost, Ann obeyed, and spent three days and three nights tending a fire on the point. Eventually, a passing boat saw the light and came to her rescue. From that point on, the cove has been named Bitter Ann's Cove.

THE PHANTOM OF JOHN TOOMER
POUCH ISLAND, BONAVISTA BAY

OFFSHORE FROM NEW-WES-VALLEY lies a rocky, windswept island. It would be like hundreds of islands that dot the coastline of Newfoundland, except for the remarkable fact that is guarded by a fiercely protective phantom. The spectre has haunted the isolated isle for generations. In the past, he has revealed himself to would-be trespassers who have dared to venture close to the island as a dark and ominous figure with the power to appear and vanish at will, leaving no sign that he been there at all.

This figure is John Toomer, the resident ghost of Pouch Island.

John Toomer died in 1869, but one of the people who keep his name alive is Robert E. Tulk, a fisherman from Newtown. Tulk learned the story of the ghost of Pouch Island from older people in the area. He says he learned that story and many others from "talking and listing to the old people telling tales."

Tulk himself has compiled many of the traditional stories from the region into a book entitled *Tales from the Kittiwake Coast*, which is published by the Kittiwake Economic Development Corporation. Some of the tales and anecdotes in his book are transcribed from oral stories, as told to the author. The source for the Pouch Island tale was Tulk's own uncle, Jim Greene.

"He was a fine storyteller," recalls Tulk.

As Uncle Jim Greene told the tale, in the years before Pouch Island was abandoned, it was inhabited by a family of the name of Toomer. Two of the Toomer brothers, James and his older brother John, owned a fishing room on the island.

While the two were brothers, they were very different. James was married, while John was a bachelor. James was easygoing and soft-spoken, while John was quick-tempered and quarrelsome. While James dreamed of leaving the island in search of a better place to live, John was ideally suited for the rugged lifestyle it demanded.

John was an excellent fisherman and hunter, and spent long hours at sea fishing, or roaming the island for seabirds. But he was also a jealous guardian of the island's natural resources. Other people avoided the Toomers' fishing grounds unless they were looking for an argument.

Life was hard on the island, and eventually, James had had enough. In 1868, he decided he would leave Pouch Island in search of a more hospitable place to build a home for his family. James went to John and asked him to accompany them, but John refused entirely. According to Tulk, "He stated in no uncertain terms that he would rather die than leave Pouch Island."

John's words proved to be prophetic, as he came down with tuberculosis and died the following winter. James and his family laid John in a cold grave on Pouch Island, and with no reason to stay, they left for good. Time passed, and the island became deserted, home only to sea birds.

Occasionally, fishermen of the area would return to Pouch Island and use it as a summer fishing station. When they did, rumours began to circulate that perhaps the island was not really deserted after all. People started to whisper that perhaps the spirit of John Toomer haunted the spot, jealously guarding his hunting and fishing grounds in death, much as he had in life.

Before long, a series of strange incidents took place which lent some weight to the local folklore. One winter, a group of hunters in an open boat got cut off from nearby Pinchard's Island by slob ice, a heavy, slushy, densely packed mass of ice fragments, snow and freezing water.

Rather than spend the night in the open boat, the hunters took shelter in a cabin located on the shores of Pouch Island. Late that night, they heard what Tulk describes as "an unholy commotion": the sound of someone, or something, hammering on the walls of the cabin. The hunters rushed outdoors, but were unable to find the source of the disturbance. A crisp layer of snow surrounded the building, and not one footprint disturbed the pristine whiteness.

That group was not the only one to encounter strange events on Pouch Island. In the winter of 1930, four hunters from Newtown went to the island to hunt for eider ducks. The four men were named Elihu Vincent, Max Melendy, Roland Tiller, and Fred Barbour.

When the foursome reached their hunting grounds, they caught sight of a lone man already onshore. Not wanting to interfere with his hunting, they set off for the western part of the island. Mysteriously, when they arrived, they found the strange figure had arrived before them. They moved on to another portion of the island, but once more found the stranger had beaten them to the spot.

One of the hunters noticed that he had not seen any other boat tied up on the island. They retraced their journey, back to where the stranger had first been spotted. The location was deserted. Like the previous hunting party, they found that there were no tracks in the snow.

As Tulk tells it, "Perplexed, they went to the other places where they had seen the lone figure. It was the same thing. No tracks. The island was deserted except for the four men."

Deserted, except for the four men and the spirit of John Toomer, still guarding the hunting grounds he loved so much.

Today, not very many people know about the Pouch Island phantom, in part because there is a shortage of old-fashioned storytellers. As Tulk says, "Most of the old people are gone now, and you know, it's a job to hear a ghost story! When the old people were around, yes, there would be no problem, but with the old people gone now, there are not many people that know about it."

The work of Robert Tulk and others ensures that the old stories will not die out completely. As long as there are people who collect and retell the tales of days gone past, phantoms like John Toomer will always have a home in Newfoundland.

THE FATAL CURSE
CHURCHILL FALLS, LABRADOR

TODAY, WHEN MOST OF US THINK of Churchill Falls, we immediately think of a huge hydroelectric project and the constant political buzz that surrounds it. Centuries ago, however, the falls were known only to native peoples who feared the roaring waters because of a terrible legend.

Churchill Falls, originally known as Grand River, starts from Ashuanipi Lake and empties into Lake Melville and drops a total of 528 metres (1,735 feet). The area was first seasonally occupied by Naskapi people. The Naskapi may have been forced onto the inhospitable hunting grounds of the Labrador plateau by pressure from the Montagnais to the south and west, and their alleged traditional enemies, the coastal Inuit.

The first known white man to see the Falls was John Maclean of the Hudson's Bay Company in 1839. When the falls were first sighted by John MacLean, he learned of a portage route around the falls and over a steep gully to a plateau, where the town of Churchill Falls would eventually be constructed. MacLean renamed the river the Hamilton River after the Newfoundland Governor Sir Charles Hamilton. It was not until 1965 that the name changed to the Churchill River in honour of Sir Winston Churchill.

In 1891, Professor C.A. Kenaston, John Montague and Henry Bryant began a journey to the natural wonder. They were hoping to receive assistance from locals who knew more about the region than they did. They were refused assistance, however, because of the indigenous belief that anyone who looked upon the Falls would die. Kenaston, Bryant and Montague managed the trip on their own, and arrived at the Falls on the second of September.

Kenaston, Bryant and Montague's expedition brought the story of a curse on the falls to an audience outside of Labrador. Over a hundred years after their exposure to the story, there are numerous versions of the legend of Churchill Falls. The *Encyclopedia of Newfoundland and Labrador* includes one short version of the tale in its entry on the Churchill River. According to that version, there were once two native maidens who went gathering wood near the falls. The unlucky pair were enticed to the edge and drawn over by an evil spirit who inhabited the waters. Since then, they have been condemned to dwell beneath the falls and work daily in servitude to the evil spirit. While they are now no longer young and beautiful, apparently they can sometimes still be seen through the mist, with outstretched arms waiting to snatch at anyone who dares to venture near the tumbling water.

The legend lives on today, and in July of 2002, I collected two additional versions of the story from two women from Churchill Falls. While both have similarities to the version printed in the *Encyclopedia*, there are a number of significant differences in them. In the more recent versions, the number of maidens has dwindled from two to one, and the idea of an evil spirit who caused the disaster has vanished.

The first of these modern versions features a less vengeful ghost. The story goes that a young maiden was hiking along the river, on a grey and misty day. Some say she was gathering berries, while others say firewood. The ground along the riverbank was quite slippery due to the spray from the falls and the rain. The maiden lost her footing, slipped into the river and plunged over the falls. While her body was never found, her spirit lived on in the water, and when the falls were running full force, her face could be seen in the falls.

The second modern version skips the details leading up to the fall, and is much more descriptive in terms of the maiden's attitude toward her tragic demise. In that version, the woman fell into the water, and ever since her death she has borne a grudge against all who visit the area. If thrill- seekers get too close, she will attempt to lure them in and keep them prisoners for eternity.

While the details of the legend have changed over the years, the sense or reputation of the falls as being cursed has lingered. One of the women who told me about the legend said that at least one, or maybe two, aircraft has crashed in the gorge when unexpected weather suddenly moved into the area.

How much truth is there to any of this? Have aircraft really crashed in the area under strange circumstances? Certainly it would be possible to sift through the aeronautical records and find out one way or the other. I would suggest, however, that it may just be a natural progression of the types of tales we tell and the way we tell them.

There is no doubt that technology has changed the face of the Churchill River and the society that lives around it. One hundred and fifty years ago, stories involving native maidens and evil spirits fit nicely into the oral tradition. Today, while the core story of the "curse" remains, it is discussed in terms of mysterious airplane accidents.

Regardless of the form the legend takes today, it is remarkable that it has survived so long. There are very few ghost stories in Newfoundland and Labrador that have such a long and continuous history. The ghostly lady of Churchill Falls has been thrilling eager listeners for generations, and will doubtlessly continue to do so for generations more.

THE LEGEND OF HOOK MAN'S POND
BAIE VERTE, BAIE VERTE PENINSULA

THE FALL OF THE YEAR HAS ARRIVED, and evening comes earlier than it has over the summer months. You stand alone by the side of the road, drawing your coat around your shoulders. The air has cooled. The darkness of the night has become more often punctuated by cold mists and fogs. Thin wispy tendrils of moisture are visible in the moonlight, reaching out like ghostly hands and twining themselves around what might be trees, or what could be rocks.

By the margin of the nearby lake the fog lays thickest, hiding the deep, still water from the view of those who drive past on the highway. Drivers and passengers alike keep their eyes on the road. This is done in part to keep watch for the dangers of the moose that are plentiful along this stretch of highway, in part to keep their minds off the other, less tangible dangers that lurk in the misty shadows beyond the safety of their cars. It is the rumour of those dangers that has brought you here.

Out of the murk by the banks of the lake emerges a tall figure. As it draws closer, it seems to be the figure of a man. His walk is unsteady, arms swinging loosely at his sides. He draws closer still and reaches out. As he does, your eyes are drawn toward an unexpected glint at the end of one gangly arm. With horror you realize the man's hand is missing, and that it has been replaced with a shiny steel hook. It is the last thing you ever see, and your screams are swallowed up by the damp fog ...

Welcome to Hook Man's Pond!

When I went digging for a good ghostly tale from the Baie Verte peninsula, it was Brian Philpott who introduced me to the legend of Hook Man's Pond. Brian Philpott is a Senior Field Engineer with the Schlumberger corporation, and is currently based in Grande Prairie, Alberta. A native of Baie Verte, Brian moved away from Newfoundland in May 2000, and has been working with Schlumberger ever since.

It was during his years growing up in Baie Verte that Brian first heard the tale of Hook Man's Pond, which is located outside of Baie Verte along Highway 410. Whether the tale of Baie Verte's Hook Man is based on fact or in folklore, it is somewhat different from other popular tales and contemporary legends involving men with hooks instead of hands.

Many readers will probably be familiar with one or more variants of the Hook Man urban legend, particularly those readers who have spent any time at all around a campfire or in a college residence. The basic premise of the urban legend is as follows. A young man and his beloved are parked in his car for a late night rendezvous. Listening to the radio they hear a news story about an escaped convict with a hook instead of a hand.

Suddenly the lovers hear a terrible scraping noise alongside the car. The lad throws the car into gear and they shoot off into the night. Later, when they arrive safely home, they are horrified to see a disembodied and bloody hook hanging from the door handle.

The origins of the hook-handed monster are not clear, but it is not an uncommon theme in modern folklore or literature. Generations of children have been introduced at an early age to the idea of a hook-wielding villain through the fictional character of Captain Hook, the piratical nemesis of Peter Pan. The Captain has been lurking around since he first appeared as a character in a play by J.M. Barrie in 1904.

Peter Pan had cut off the hand of the pirate captain in battle. In its place the pirate had fixed a sharp hook, which added to his terrible appearance. As Barrie describes him, "his eyes were of the blue of the forget-me-not, and of a profound melancholy, save when he was plunging his hook into you, at which time two red spots appeared in them and lit them up horribly."

Unlike Captain Hook, the Hook Man of Baie Verte legend lost his hand in some unspecified manner for some unspecified reason. As Brian puts it, the hero of our story "lost his hand years before ... why or how I do not know."

Steel hook firmly in place, the man set off for a drive one night along Highway 410, leaving Baie Verte behind. Along his route, the one-handed driver hit a bump in the road. He lost control of the vehicle and it went spinning off the road. The car rolled down the embankment and eventually came to rest in a nearby pond. The man, injured in the accident, was for some reason unable to extricate himself from the wreck. Water poured in around him, and trapped in the car, the man drowned.

The story, of course, does not end there. The accident happened in the fall of the year on a foggy evening in the mid- to late 1970s. Since then, on similarly foggy fall evenings, people have claimed to see the figure of a man walking the highway near the pond. The legend became so entrenched in local folklore that some people even began to refer to the pond itself as Hook Man's Pond.

One of the more intriguing parts of the tale involves the bump in the road that was responsible for the original fateful accident. The legend maintains that the bump was repaired several times by the Department of Works, Services and Transportation.

The mysterious lump in the tarmac always returned, as often as it was removed. Whether this was due to some eerie paranormal force, natural causes, or questionable skills of the repair crews remains an unsolved mystery of its own. As Brian tells it, "it always reappeared and is probably still there."

If you happen to been one of those who have seen the ghostly figure, or have further information on his sad history, more information is always appreciated. If you have not seen him, think twice before you rush out to try to spot him for yourself. Locals in the know claim that one should not drive pass Hook Man's Pond on a foggy evening, lest you see Mr. Hook Man and have an accident of your own.

Bibliography

Arrowsmith, Nancy. <u>A Field Guide to the Little People.</u> New York: Hill and Wang, 1977.

"A Strange Story." <u>St. John's Woman</u> June 1963: 51.

"A True Ghost Story." <u>St. John's Woman</u> October 1962: 14–16.

Bennett, Margaret. <u>The Last Stronghold.</u> St. John's: Breakwater, 1989.

"Capt. Randell Tells a 'Ghost' Story." <u>The Fishermen's Advocate</u> July 16, 1929, p. 6.

Chambers, Paul. <u>Sex and the Paranormal.</u> London: Blandford, 1999.

Coish, Calvin. "Newfoundland's Pirates: The Jolly Roger and Pieces of Eight." <u>Atlantic Advocate</u> 73.2 (1982): 42–47.

Colombo, John Robert. <u>Ghost Stories of Canada.</u> Toronto: Dundurn P, 2000.

Cordingly, David. <u>Under the Black Flag: The Romance and the Reality of Life Among the Pirates.</u> New York: Random House, 1996.

D. "The Ghost in Gov't House. Is the Vice-Regal Mansion Haunted?" The Newfoundland Herald TV Week January 18, 1978: 52.

Encyclopedia of Newfoundland and Labrador. CD-ROM Version 1.2. St. John's: Harry Cuff Publications Limited, 1998.

Fitzgerald, Jack. Ghosts, Heroes and Oddities. St. John's: Jesperson Press, 1991.

Fitzgerald, Jack. Jack Fitzgerald's Notebook. St. John's: Creative Publishers, 1985.

Fitzgerald, Jack. Where Angels Fear to Tread. St. John's: Creative Publishers, 1995.

Galgay, Frank and Michael McCarthy. Buried Treasure of Newfoundland and Labrador. St. John's: Harry Cuff Publications, 1989.

Galgay, Frank and Michael McCarthy. Shipwrecks of Newfoundland and Labrador. Vol 3. St. John's: Creative Publishers, 1995.

A Gift of Heritage: Historic Architecture of St. John's. 2nd Edition. St. John's: Newfoundland Historic Trust, 1997.

Hervey, Sheila. Canada Ghost to Ghost. Toronto: Stoddart, 1996.

"The Hills of Home." Newfoundland Herald TV Week. May 10, 1978: 60.

Holzer, Hans. Ghosts: True Encounters with the World Beyond. New York: Black Dog and Leventhal Publishers, 1997.

Howley, Rev. M. F. "Newfoundland Name Lore Part XXVIII." The Newfoundland Quarterly 9.3 (1909): 9-10.

Hufford, D.J. The Terror that Comes in the Night: An Experience-Centered Study of Supernatural Assault Traditions. Philadelphia: U of Pennsylvania P, 1982.

J.V. "The Ghost in Simpson's Bar." The Newfoundland Herald TV Week September 13, 1978: 87.

Keegan, Nora Healey. Footprints in the Sand. Jesperson Printing Ltd., 1979.

Kinsella, R.J. Some Superstitions and Traditions of Newfoundland. 1919.

Newfoundland Historic Trust. A Gift of Heritage. 2nd Ed. St. John's: Newfoundland Historic Trust, 1997.

O'Neill, Paul The Story of St. John's Newfoundland. Vol 1 & 2. Erin, ON: Press Porcepic, 1976.

Parsons, Robert. Survive the Savage Seas: Tales from our Ocean Heritage. St. John's: Creative Publishers, 1998.

Pilgrim, Earl B. The Ghost of Ellen Dower. St. John's: Flanker Press, 2002.

"The Pirates Cobham." New Land Magazine (Autumn 1964): 13- 19.

Pitt, David G. Windows of Agates: The Life and Times of Gower Street Church, St. John's, Newfoundland 1815-1990. St. John's, Jesperson P, 1990.

"Port in a Storm" (undated manuscript), attachment to personal communication from Henry Collingwood, Baine, Johnston & Co. Ltd., August 26, 1998. Heritage Foundation of Newfoundland and Labrador unnumbered file "St. John's - Newman Wine Vaults."

Resident. "The Drowned Man of Fogo." The Newfoundland Herald TV Week July 5, 1978: 37.

Rogonzinski, Jan. The Wordsworth Dictionary of Pirates. New York: Facts on File, 1995.

Seymour, John and Harry Neligan. True Irish Ghost Stories. Dublin: Hodges, Figgis and Company, 1926.

Story, G. M., W. J. Kirwin, and J. D .A. Widdowson, eds. Dictionary of Newfoundland English. Toronto: U of Toronto P, 1982.

"The Ship the Devil Towed." New Land Magazine (Summer-Autumn, 1962): 13-15.

The Story and Origin of Hunt, Roope & Company, London and Oporto, Newman, Hunt & Company, Londan, Newman & Company, Newfoundland 1395-1951. London: Hunt, Roope and Company Ltd., 1951.

Thomas, Gerald. The Two Traditions: The Art of Storytelling Amongst French Newfoundlanders. St. John's: Breakwater, 1993.

Thoms, James R. God is our Guide: A Brief History of the District Grand Lodge of Newfoundland and the United Grand Lodge of Ancient, Free and Accepted Masons of England. St. John's: District Grand Lodge of Newfoundland, 1970.

Wakeham, P.J. "Ghost Stories." New Land Magazine 17 (1970): 61-63.

Wakeham, P.J. "Newfoundland Ghostly Legends." New Land Magazine 35 (Spring/Summer 1979): 49-51.

White, Jack A. Streets of St. John's. St. John's: Creative Publishers, 1989.

White, Jack A. Streets of St. John's. Vol. Three. St. John's: Creative Publishers, 1992.

White, John W. "Ferryland (What Doth Not Appear in History)." The Newfoundland Quarterly 1.4 (1902): 11-12.

White, William. "Ghosts and Phantom Lights." The Trinitarian Christmas Number, December 1925.

Wilson, Colin and John Grant. The Directory of Possibilities. Rutledge P: New York, 1981.

Dale Gilbert Jarvis is a performer, researcher, writer and storyteller living and working in St. John's. He holds a B.Sc. (Honours) in Anthropology from Trent University and an MA in Folklore from Memorial University of Newfoundland. He currently works for the Heritage Foundation of Newfoundland and Labrador, and is President of the Newfoundland Historic Trust. Dale is a regular writer for and contributor to *The Downhomer Magazine*, and his fortnightly exploration of all things paranormal in the province, "Newfoundland Unexplained," is a regular column in *The Telegram*.

As a storyteller, Dale has performed locally and at international festivals, but is perhaps less well known than his alter ego, the distinguished Reverend Thomas Wyckham Jarvis, Esquire. Since 1997, The Reverend has been the host and guide of the St. John's Haunted Hike, a walking ghost tour through the haunted streets of St. John's. Under his supervision, locals and tourists have been introduced to the vengeful lovers, murdered soldiers, and mysterious fires which await those brave enough to explore the secrets that lie in wait in St. John's darkest corners. Mixing history, humour, and traditional storytelling, Dale has been winning over audiences and throwing in the odd scare here and there, and has been covered by a wide variety of local, national and international media.

Dale lives in an old yellow row house in downtown St. John's with his partner Kelly Jones, their four cats, and a relatively helpful ghost.

Places Visited by the Paranormal

Arnold's Cove
Baie Verte
Barachois Brook
Bishops Falls
Bitter Ann's Cove
Black Duck Brook
Bonavista
Boxey
Branch
Buchans
Burgeo
Cartwright
Chaleur Bay
Chance Cove
Chapel Cove
Churchill Falls
Clarke's Beach
Cobb's Arm
Codroy Valley
Conception Bay
Conception Bay South
Conche
Corner Brook
Fogo
Fortune Bay
Georgestown
Goulds

Grand Codroy River
Hall's Bay
Harbour Grace
Holyrood
Kelly's Island
Lewisporte
Little Colinet Island
Lolly Cove
London, England
Milton
Mount Pearl
Northern Bay Sands
Petty Harbour
Port de Grave
Port Union
Pouch Cove, B.B.
Random Island
Rocky Harbour
St. John's
St. Lawrence
St. Shott's
St. Vincent's
Seldom Come By
Shoe Cove Bight
Swift Current
Table Bay
Trinity